MID-CENTURY

MODERN

MID-CENTURY

FURNITURE OF THE 1950s BY CARA GREENBERG

NEW PHOTOGRAPHY BY TIM STREET-PORTER

DESIGNED BY GEORGE CORSILLO

HARMONY BOOKS/NEW YORK

In loving memory of my parents, Joseph and Rhoda Rogoff

Published by Harmony Books, a division of Crown Publishers, Inc., 201 East 50th Street, New York, New York 10022. Member of the Crown Publishing Group.

Random House, Inc. New York, Toronto, London, Sydney, Auckland

Originally published in hardcover by Harmony Books, a division of Crown Publishers, Inc., in 1984.

HARMONY and colophon are trademarks of Crown Publishers, Inc.

Manufactured in Singapore

Library of Congress Cataloging-in-Publication Data
Greenberg, Cara.
Mid-century modern.
1. Furniture—History—20th century. I. Title.
TS885.G68 1984 683.1'09'045 84-3777
ISBN 0-517-88475-5

10 9 8 7 6 5 4 3 2 1

First Revised Edition

FOREWORD

OCCASIONALLY YOU'LL HEAR someone say that '50s furniture is having a "resurgence." That's no fleeting blip of cheap nostalgia we're seeing. Furniture from the '50s has been "resurging" for at least fifteen years now—and it shows no signs of abating.

There are few things about which one can make so certain a pronouncement of immortality as a George Nelson platform bench or Noguchi table. When something attains that level of design purity and sculptural assuredness, it is bound to remain popular, and to be rediscovered again and again by each new generation.

Designer Paul Frankl once wrote: "Style is the external expression of the inner spirit of any given time." As it turns out, the exuberant style of the mid-century had more staying power than anyone imagined. Its boundaries were not hard-edged, with an arbitrary cut-off line at 1960. Instead, it is enduring heartily into the next millennium, still defining modernism for our age. Its prototypical curve—the relaxed parabola that describes the trajectory of a rocket—was not just the cutting edge of a single decade, but an overarching form language that symbolizes the better part of a century.

The frank construction and eccentric shapes of the 1950s that once caused scoffing in scholarly circles no longer appear outrageous. In light of the post-modernist whimsies and brutal deconstructionism of the 1980s, '50s furniture seems, in fact, refined.

That demand for this kind of furniture has soared is reflected in the number of new stores around the country that specialize in vintage furnishings of the period. The source guide at the back of this book has swelled from just a few to nearly seventy retail outlets. They range from hushed galleries where European desks and cabinets bear six-figure price tags to lively jumbles of the wire, ply-wood, and fiberglass that distinguished the domestic output of the day.

Another telling indication of growing interest is the recent reissue by the Herman Miller Company—after years of being besieged by customer requests—of nine classic pieces representing the apex of '50s design in America. When this book was written eleven years ago, many of the icons championed herein were costly and hard to find. I remember my chagrin, a few years back, in spotting an Eames elliptical "surfboard" table late one night in the window of a Brooklyn antiques shop, then rushing back for it first thing the next morning—and finding it gone. I need no longer kick myself for that one. As of last year, that table can be had, not a line off the original (although purists would argue that the new ones lack whatever patina laminated plywood acquires), for about $700, or one-third the going price for a vintage example.

Since this book appeared, many of the important figures whose work is celebrated here have died. I feel fortunate in having been able to interview George Nelson for this book, and to have had tea and conversation with Ray Eames at Manhattan's Stanhope Hotel. The fact that they—along with Isamu Noguchi and others—are gone adds historical import to their designs in the same way a painter's work increases in value when it's certain there won't be any more forthcoming.

With our comfortable four decades of hindsight, the best of mid-century furniture stands out more than ever for its artistry and integrity. The leading lights of '50s furniture design reached so deep into the what, why, and how of people's furniture needs—including the need for visual delight—that they touched something elemental. Those needs, both practical and aesthetic, change little with the passage of time. Like the great rock 'n' roll of the same era, '50s furniture is here to stay.

—Cara Greenberg
March 1995

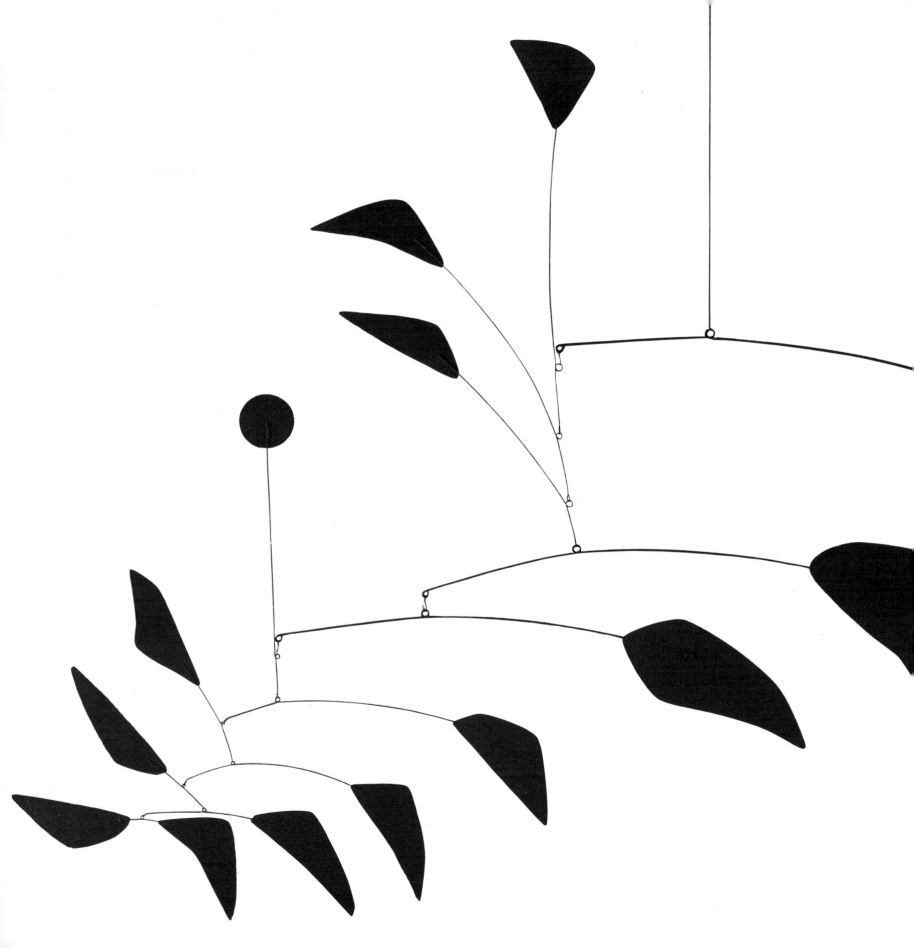

CONTENTS

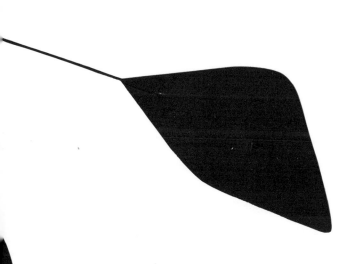

HERE WERE YOU IN '52?

I know where I was . . . in a crib painted with yellow duckies, underneath the casement windows of a newly built apartment house in Queens, New York. Out in the living room, a few pieces of furniture proclaimed us a family of modern-design consciousness, if limited means. There were a couple of wrought-iron chairs slung with canvas pouches (2 of 5 million sold), a low slat bench on which rested a bulky, wooden cube of a TV, and an early example of a storage wall, constructed by my father (a shop teacher) and painted by my mother (a reader of decorating magazines) in the then fashionable shade of forest green. We had a Modigliani print of a girl with an improbably long neck, a spun-aluminum pendant lamp over a blond wood, vaguely Scandinavian dining table, a straw rug on the floor, and little else.

In their urge toward "modern," my parents were no different from millions of other ex-GIs and their brides. It suited young families, after all, this spare and simple decor. It was comfortable, child-proof, and scaled to fit smaller postwar houses and apartments. It was lightweight and easily moved, across the room or out to the suburbs. It didn't necessarily cost a lot, and it didn't have to be bought in suites. Above all, it was stylish. Having modern furniture instead of traditional

in 1946 or 1949 or 1952 proved you were *au courant*.

Good taste or bad, highbrow or low, the members of our parents' generation—those who dwelt behind plate-glass picture windows in the Connecticut woods as well as the multitudes in the cookie-cutter split levels of suburbia—were all motivated by the same desire: to escape the stuffy, old-fashioned rooms of their own youths and to be, as every young generation wants to be, and is, by definition, "modern."

The word *modern* has always meant the same thing—of the moment—but exactly what *modern* meant in the late 1940s and 1950s was not, of course, what it had ever meant before. Modern architecture was steel-and-glass skyscrapers and flat-roofed California-style houses with walls of glass and fieldstone fireplaces. The modern art scene was spattered with the abstract expressionist paintings of Jackson Pollack and the free-floating mobiles of Alexander Calder. The progressive hi-fi played Thelonius Monk and Charlie Parker.

In furniture, modern came in all price brackets. Those who could afford it filled architect-designed homes with furniture from smart department stores which, in those days, promoted furniture even more vigorously than fashion. A sophisticated home of the early Fifties might have featured, for example, a pair of Eero Saarinen's all-enveloping Womb chairs in bright red, or had as its *pièce de résistance* the free-form walnut-and-glass coffee table of Isamu Noguchi, its sculptured two-part base subject to rearrangement at its owner's whim.

At its high end, the period from 1945 to 1960 was a heyday for furniture. From VJ Day to JFK, the furniture industry had everything going for it: top designers to design a new product, new technologies to make it, an eager press to promote it, and an affluent public to buy it. They were years of unusual brazenness and adventurousness for the world design community. For a brief span of a decade and a half, mass-produced furniture reached a design pinnacle achieved neither before nor since.

The best of it was designed by architects who, during the war, when nobody was building houses, had turned their talents to furniture—or who, in desperation for furnishings that made sense in the smaller, sparer postwar house, decided to design their own.

Architect/designers Charles Eames, George Nelson, Eero Saarinen, Arne Jacobsen, Giò Ponti, and others brought to the most domestic of the decorative arts their uniquely integrated way of viewing a piece of furniture in its context—within a room, within a house. Out of this approach came pieces that have places assured in the pantheon of great furniture, right alongside those of prewar design giants Le Corbusier, Miës van der Rohe, and Marcel Breuer. The mid-century designers certainly deserve front-row seats. Even today, their best efforts refuse to look dated.

Ironically, the Fifties is not commonly remembered for its monuments to modernism. The characteristic bad taste of the period had an amusing vulgarity that is not easily forgotten. The other side of the taste coin, the screaming kitsch look, left the decade's decor with an undeservedly tarty reputation. Later, growing up on Long Island, I ran into some outstanding proponents of the harlequin wallpaper/gold-flecked lampshades/fake bonsai tree set.

If it wasn't flat-out hideous, cheap, and mass-produced Fifties furniture was often just clunky. The groundbreaking designs were quickly followed by waves of uninspired knock-offs—uncomfortable flat-slab sofas, coffee tables by the millions mimicking the amoeba, the boomerang, and the human kidney, boxy blond night tables topped with motel-room lamps. By their sheer number, they have tended to obscure the fact that brilliance in furniture design was more typical of the postwar decade than mediocrity.

Reviving the reputation of the 1940s and '50s as extraordinary years for furniture is the point of this book. The popular culture of the period, already much vaunted, needs no further celebrating. That said, the fact that the Fifties was, after all, the decade that gave us Elvis, Chuck Berry, the drive-in, and the barbecue can't be *completely* ignored. If a few items or interiors of questionable pedigree have slipped in among the classics, it's because they have their places as icons of a changing culture. Those starburst chandeliers, atom clocks, and boomerang tables have become beloved symbols of a simpler, more straightforward time, when

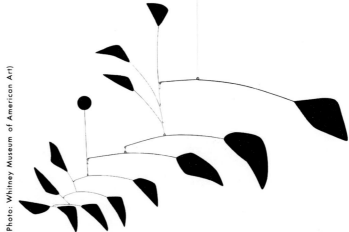

(Photo: Whitney Museum of American Art)

"BIG RED," MOBILE/ ALEXANDER CALDER/ 1959
The free forms of Calder's air-directed mobiles echoed shapes that appeared as post-war table tops and swoopy sofas.

■The avant-garde postwar house, with its characteristic spareness and light-weight, industrially inspired furnishings —such as this vacation home in Washington State, designed and furnished by architect Wendell Lovett—bore little resemblance to the self-consciously glamorous "moderne" interiors of the 1930s.

options were fewer, sex roles clear cut, atomic energy still a positive idea, and anxiety not so pervasive.

But the emphasis is decidedly on the work of the masters and their fiendishly clever, strikingly attractive solutions to the mid-century design problem: how to use terrific advances in manufacturing technology and a host of new materials to fill the furniture needs of consumers—without sacrificing the artistry and spirit of the designer.

I hope this book will change the minds of those who were so blinded by the glare of pole lamps on Formica bar tops that they have failed to realize the finer side of late '40s and '50s furniture. For those who don't need to be convinced, I hope this book will foster new appreciation for the refined good taste of the Danes, the fabulous flamboyance of the Italians, and the technical wizardry of the Americans; refocus eyes on the pliable imaginings of the postwar furniture designers and will put some of those who have faded unfairly into obscurity back on their pedestals.

The symbol ⌐ appearing with a caption indicates that the piece shown is in current production. A source guide to manufacturers and distributors is on page 169.

⌐ **SLING CHAIR/JORGE FERRARI-HARDOY/1938**
It embodies all the advantages of the Mid-Century Modern chair—good-looking, lightweight, inexpensive—and it has become the one chair, by its very ubiquitousness, to convey "Fifties" to the generation to follow.
(Photo: Knoll International)

(Photo: Knoll International)

■A Norman Rockwell cover for the *Saturday Evening Post* starring the Womb chair.

➴ WOMB CHAIR/EERO SAARINEN/ 1948

Saarinen dubbed this the Womb chair because of the way you could curl up in it. Its commodious contours were perfect for the casual body language of the slouching, sprawling Fifties.

➴ COFFEE TABLE/ISAMU NOGUCHI/ 1944

Focal point of a stylish mid-century living room: sculptor Isamu Noguchi's coffee table, manufactured through 1972 by Herman Miller, discontinued, then reintroduced in 1984. A movable base of walnut supports a triangular plate-glass top.

MODERNE BECOMES MODERN

The early 1950s was not the first time modern furniture had been offered to the American public, but it was the first time they lined up around the block to buy it. Buy they did, with the hard cash of postwar prosperity, driven by a sudden, voracious hunger for curves that were swoopy, parabolic, amoeboid; lines that were long and low; ornament that was absent; materials that, until recently, had been found only in aircraft factories.

Modern had become a buzz word. For a few years, from the late '40s to the late '50s, the tastemaking press honeymooned with the concept. Magazines, newspapers, department stores, even home economics teachers were all in agreement: modern furnishings were the right look for the new age.

But what *was* modern furniture? Hadn't it been tried before the war and not caught on?

True, the style being called modern and milked with such relish had actually been in existence for more than two decades, but it had never been particularly accessible—or acceptable—to the consumer. The Bauhaus visionaries Ludwig Miës van der Rohe and Marcel Breuer and the Swiss-born architect Charles Edouard Jeanneret (Le Corbusier) had outlined in the 1920s and '30s, with astonishing prescience, the forms Fifties furniture was to follow. These men—architects

LOUNGE CHAIR/MARCEL BREUER/ 1935–36
Early organic: Breuer's laminated plywood lounge, manufactured by the English firm Isokon, was a translation from aluminum and one of the first pieces to suggest the flow of living tissue.

(Photo: The Museum of Modern Art)

◢ WASSILY CHAIR/MARCEL BREUER/ 1925

Out of the Bauhaus came the first classic chair of the twentieth century and the first tubular steel chair designed for residential use. The Wassily incorporated the influences of earlier movements—the boxy shape of the Cubists, the intersecting planes of de Stijl and the exposed framework of the Constructivists.

◢ BASCULANT CHAIR/LE CORBUSIER & CHARLOTTE PERRIAND/1928

Named after the seesaw, this early exercise in tubular steel and calf hide had a pivoting backrest, a feature made much of in later chairs. Its right-angled rigidity did not survive into the loosened-up Fifties.

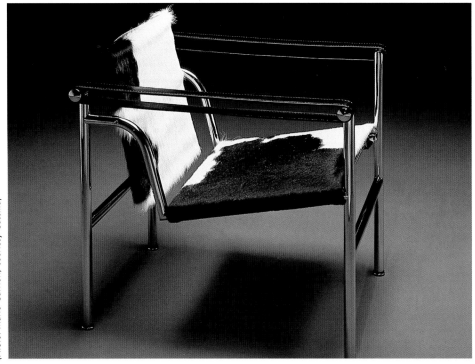

(Photo: Mario Carrieri, courtesy Cassina)

for whom furniture design was a captive extension of their greater art—had made a complete break with reactionary "period" furniture styles. Their furniture made no apologies for its machine origins. The clean, pure lines of their tubular steel and bent plywood chairs established a new aesthetic, proving that beauty was not the exclusive province of the craftsman.

Its appearance was radically minimal after the excesses of Victoriana, its construction superbly polished. "Form follows function" was a Bauhaus motto, and, in some respects, chairs such as Breuer's Wassily and Miës van der Rohe's Barcelona functioned very well. But if a chair's purpose is to be comfortable, then the commitment to function of modern furniture of the 1920s and '30s was not always overriding. Elegance usually won out. Americans of the time found Bauhaus-type furniture forbiddingly icy and in any case, during the Depression, could not afford to buy it.

As for the patrician furniture of exotic woods and fine workmanship that is the only rightful heir to the name Art Deco, it was not truly a forerunner of the style the media of the Fifties would call modern. Although the cabinetry of Süe et Mare and Emile-Jacques Ruhlmann, Art Deco's leading practitioners, had pleasing clean lines, such furniture had more in common with what came before than after—painstaking expressions of luxury and wealth. Art Deco was not furniture for the machine age. It never intended to be affordable, and never was.

The one successful, popularly priced exception to the dearth of modern furniture in pre–World War II America was the Conant Ball Company's Modern Living line of 1935, designed by Russel Wright, a vociferous early champion of modern furniture for the masses. Though bulky and inelegant, each item of solid maple furniture in the line could be purchased individually and arranged by the buyer in flexible groupings, a stupendous notion at the time. The line

MR CHAIR/MIËS VAN DER ROHE/ 1926
All-in-one elegance: the first successful cantilevered chair in tubular steel—a miracle of resiliency, simplicity, strength, and lightness.

also featured the first widely available sectional couch. It was an instant, enormous hit, not to be repeated in the 1930s, either by Wright, who then turned his attention to ceramics, or by any other prewar modern furniture designer in this country.

Through the '30s, America excelled in modern *industrial* design. Raymond Loewy, Norman Bel Geddes, Henry Dreyfuss, and Walter Dorwin Teague produced streamlined wares of every description, both for corporations and consumers. Gas pumps, clocks, vacuum cleaners, typewriters, pencil sharpeners, refrigerators, and ranges—not to mention cars, trains, ships, and planes—all eschewed the ornamentation of yore for a long, clean line, curved at the end to suggest speed, which was the essence and symbol of modernity.

But furniture hadn't met with the same good fortune as toasters and radios. Despite a small circle of American designers who created extraordinary modern furniture before World War II—notably Gilbert Rohde, Kem Weber, Paul Frankl, and Donald Deskey—the average prewar home was furnished with "Grand Rapids borax," a contemporary term for ill-designed and poorly con-

structed mass-market furniture that substituted applied "motifs" and complicated carving to mask total lack of understanding of the interrelationship of form and function.

All across the land, there were overstuffed mohair living room suites, "waterfall" bedroom suites, and so-called modernistic suites which featured unnecessary zigzags and "skyscraper" detailing in lame imitation of the flourishing French decorative arts of the day.

Or else the living room was an unabashed throwback to eighteenth-century Europe. Convinced that Europe was synonymous with "culture" and America with "barbarism," homeowners unsure of their powers of discrimination, and with little idea of what indigenous American furniture would look like, anyhow, tried to reassure themselves with heavy velvet curtains, Louis-the-something chairs, mahogany highboys, and brocade-covered walls. There was mock Italian Renaissance, mock Gothic, mock Chippendale, and mock Queen Anne—stifling it was. Would America's living rooms ever breathe again?

LIVING ROOM/RUSSEL WRIGHT/ 1935

Mass-market fodder, Russel Wright's Modern Living furniture line for the Conant Ball Company was basically rectilinear, with rounded edges and corners. Comfortingly solid yet unmistakably modern, it scored a huge hit with Depression-era customers.

DINING ROOM/GILBERT ROHDE/ 1934

As good as American Art Deco got were Rohde's urbane designs for Herman Miller. The cantilevered tubular steel chairs owe a big debt to the 1920s designs of Mart Stam and Marcel Breuer.

➤ ARMCHAIR/ALVAR AALTO/1934
The Finnish designer's master stroke, and a sensation at the 1939 New York World's Fair. The broad, continuous curve of the seat and bent plywood arms achieved a winning combination of comfort, lightness, and grace.

VISIONS OF TOMORROW

The 1939 New York World's Fair proved to be that much-needed breath of fresh air. In the model houses invariably called "homes of tomorrow," people got a tantalizing glimpse of what was to come. What they saw at Flushing Meadows that prewar summer, and the next, stimulated their imaginations, raised their design consciousnesses, and conditioned them, for the first time, to think of modern furniture as something that perhaps they *could* live with, graciously and sensibly—instead of as furniture designed just for an artsy few, or furniture that was part of a passing fad.

Much of what they saw and liked were reflections of things that had already been unveiled at European fairs—Stockholm, 1930; Brussels, 1935, and Paris, 1937—ideas that would later be translated by American furniture makers into native dialect. In the Finnish pavilion, they went wild for the bent plywood armchairs of Alvar Aalto, including the first-ever chair with a continuous, one-piece curved plywood back and seat. The French showed crisp, fresh model rooms featuring furniture with softly tapering legs, which flowed in wide yet controlled curves, chairs covered in zebra skin, and more blond wood. The Dutch astonished everyone with double- triple-, quadruple-duty furniture—single cabinets incorporating desk, bookcase, radio/phonograph, *and* storage for dishes.

At the same time fairgoers were viewing the modern furnishings of Europe, they were being dazzled by optimistic projections for the future at the fair's main exhibits—superhighways traveled by teardrop-shaped cars at General Motors's Futurama, simulated space flights at Rocketport of the Future, a harmonious life of leisure and fulfillment at the Democracity panorama inside the Perisphere—all promised by 1960. The 1939 fair set the stage for the postwar success of modern furniture by instilling in people a fantasy they would later try to live out by furnishing their homes in a futuristic way.

ORGANIC MODELS

Tomorrow arrived all too soon, and it wasn't what it had been cracked up to be. In fact, it was wartime, and the furniture industry was an early casualty. In Europe, it died completely. In this country, a few manufacturers persevered in spite of materials shortages and manufacturing restrictions.

But despite world events, 1940 did not turn out to be a bad year for achievement in furniture design. That year, The Museum of Modern Art in New York announced its Organic Design in Home Furnishings competition, an event meant to rout out new design talent that might be lurking in the hinterlands. The contest was a brilliant success. Out of the woodwork came Charles Eames and Eero Saarinen, two young architects associated with Michigan's Cranbrook Academy. They took top honors in both contest categories—seating and storage—and it is safe to say that furniture was never the same again.

Their entries even redefined the meaning of the contest. While the consortium of retailers and manufacturers sponsoring it had intended the word *organic* to signify unity or wholeness within a decorative scheme, the dramatic group of plywood shell chairs Eames and Saarinen proposed—including a sexy trio called Conversation, Relaxation, and Lounging—were organic in every way. Here, in an early incarnation, was the free-form, sculptural quality—the protoplasmic blobbishness—that was to become a hallmark of the furniture of the postwar period. Their easy, fluid shapes seemed almost to have personality, and they were clearly designed with the spine in mind. Instead of sinking into these chairs, as one did with conventional upholstered furniture, they offered continuous support from the moment the body made contact with their firm plywood curves. Eames and Saarinen had used plywood veneers in a revolutionary way, pressing it, layer by layer, into a complex series of multidimensional curves that superseded the two-dimensional world of bent plywood pioneered in the 1930s by Alvar Aalto.

The Eames/Saarinen chairs were outstanding for technology as well as for design. They became prototypes for much of what was to follow in the next two decades—prototypes in a spiritual sense at least, for none of the chairs were ever produced in their 1940 forms. In the process of manufacturing (which was not to happen until the war ended five years later), their purely sculptural essences had to be tamed a bit. But as a statement of new direction in furniture design, the Eames/Saarinen entries were loud and clear.

The team's winning storage units were no less innovative for their time. There were benches and cases, some with shelves, some with drawers, and some with doors. Plain and rectilinear as could be, they carried the idea of flexibility in use further than any group of furniture had yet done. Even the drawers were interchangeable from one piece to the next.

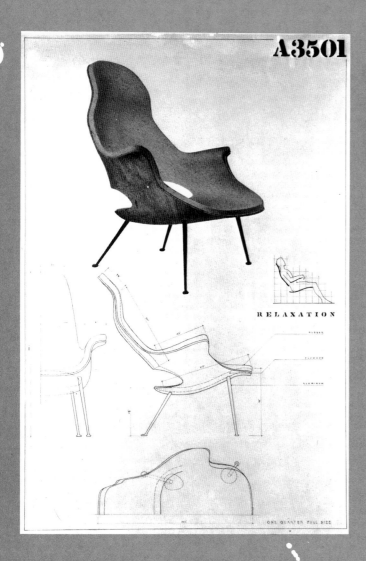

A3501

RELAXATION

ONE QUARTER FULL SIZE

A3501

CONVERSATION

THICKNESS OF PLYWOOD VARIES
WITH STRUCTURAL DEMANDS

ONE QUARTER FULL SIZE

A3501

The prototypes that launched "organic modernism," products of the two greatest imaginations in postwar furniture design. Three of ten designs submitted to The Museum of Modern Art's Organic Design in Home Furnishings contest, they were radical both in form and in proposed manufacturing technology.
(Photos: The Museum of Modern Art)

LOUNGING SHAPE

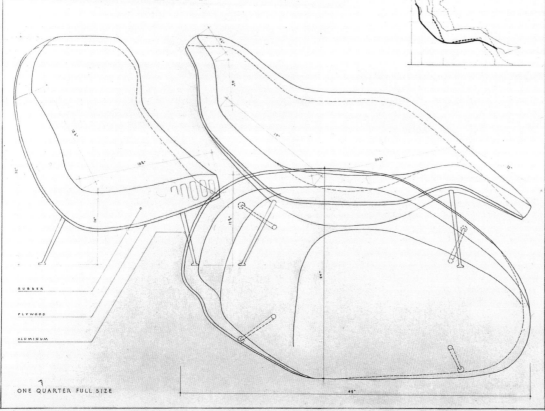

RUBBER

PLYWOOD

ALUMINUM

ONE QUARTER FULL SIZE

■Furniture that loved to be mass-produced: Eames plastic shell chairs on the assembly line in Zeeland, Michigan. Round rubber "shock mounts" on the chair's underside were the liaison between the molded fiberglass and the metal legs—an innovation of wartime technology.

(Photo: Herman Miller)

LOUNGE CHAIR/CHARLES EAMES/ c. 1944

Charles and Ray Eames's experiments with plywood molding techniques led to this experimental lounge, a clear forerunner of the mid-'50s leather-and-rosewood classic. Three large wraparound pieces of molded ply received the sitter's body generously. The cantilevered steel tubing base was designed to tilt back and absorb the occupant's energy. It was never produced, because it was large and expensive.

(Photo: The Museum of Modern Art)

NEW MATERIALS

Oddly enough, the organically shaped furniture inspired by the museum's contest models was going to be manufactured out of a stunning array of inorganic substances, the by-products of wartime research and development in the heavy industries. In fact, without the war, the look of the Fifties would not have been possible.

From the aircraft industry came new ways of molding plastics and aluminum as an option for furniture design. New methods of molding and laminating plywood were derived from experiments that Charles Eames and his wife, Ray, conducted around 1942 for the U.S. Navy, when they were looking for ways to make lightweight, stackable leg splints. The Chrysler Corporation developed spot-welding techniques for joining wood to metal, rubber, and plastic. Fiberglass, cast aluminum, acrylics, polyester resins, foam rubber—a plethora of lightweight, durable, maintenance-free materials entered the design vocabulary.

One thing was certain: the World War II materials and technology revolution changed forever the aesthetic basis on which furniture would be judged. It no longer made any sense to ask, "How well crafted is it?" because it wasn't designed to be crafted at all, but fabricated by machine—at the lowest possible cost and in great numbers. Elaborate carving and painstaking handiwork were out, for the present. And fiberglass was about as removed as you could get from amboyna and ivory, materials doted on in the Art Deco era, so there was no point comparing them.

DRAWING/HARVEY PROBBER/ 1941
This designer's sketch—the winning entry in a magazine competition titled "Interiors to Come"—shows that the hallmarks of the postwar look in modern furnishings were percolating in the minds of young designers even during the war: free-form and crescent-shape seating, long, low storage, and a generally wide-open use of space.
(Courtesy of the designer)

THE NEW MODERNISM

Although the machine look in furniture had been around in the 1930s, and the use of plastics was not totally foreign, acceptance of the *new* modernism required another leap of faith, for the shapes that started to emerge in the late '40s took the old Bauhaus dictates a step further.

The machine age in furniture had moved into its next phase—it had gotten off the ground. While a long, curved line may have sufficed to describe the movement of the *Wabash Cannonball* or the *Queen Mary*, it was the parabolic trajectory of a jet plane or rocket that was the dominant line of the Forties and Fifties. A new age of aerospace was beginning, and furniture would reflect it exuberantly.

It was a bit shocking at first, this strangely shaped new furniture. It looked utterly different from what most people were used to living with. Some never caught on, like Mrs. G. Magnon Crowe in a 1951 book, *Good Taste Costs No More*, by Richard Gump.

"I'm looking for a table," she says, entering a furniture department.

"Traditional or Modern?" asks the salesman.

"Oh, not Modern!" she gasps.

But even those with a burgeoning taste for modern needed help, which the home furnishings magazines, looking for upbeat copy, were only too happy to provide. Through the war, they published articles along the lines of "Planning Your Peacetime Decorating" and were vigorous exponents of (usually) good design in modern furniture.

A few architecture student types bent *way* over in their eagerness to embrace the new ideas. Their early attempts at decorating with modern furniture tended to have what George Nelson called a "manifesto quality." Writing later about the avant-garde camps of the early 1940s, Nelson said, "In the raging battle between conservatism and modernism, the battalions in the front lines of progress had to have their banners—the symbols included monk's cloth, Miró reproductions, Aalto chairs, and Calder mobiles." (Or, more likely, homemade mobiles à la Calder.)

At that time, though, the furniture industry was moribund and inventory in the stores scanty. Questions of taste and connoisseurship were mostly cocktail party exercises, but at least it took people's minds off the war.

TABLE & CHAIRS/CHARLES EAMES/1950s

Archetypes of the Fifties' family—harried commuter, housecoated housewife, and boom babies—populate this c.1957 advertising shot showing how Eames's plastic shell chairs and cast-aluminum-based Formica table could work in a domestic setting.

■The Carson, Pirie, Scott department store's home planning center, in those prehistoric days when women made careers out of decorating their own homes, was furnished with a variety of Eames shell chairs. This ad for its services ran in the *Chicago Daily News* in 1954.

■"The house is a machine for living," said Le Corbusier. "But only insofar as the heart of a man is a suction pump," Frank Lloyd Wright added. In this tongue-in-cheek view of the results of the application of unsullied modernist theory, the children of the house/machine have discovered a function unimagined by the architect at his drawing board.
(Illustration: Mary Petty from *Homes of the Brave*, T. H. Robsjohn-Gibbings, 1954)

THE NEW MENTALITY

It had taken the war to get America out of the Depression, and the end of war for its citizens to be able to enjoy it. A sense of relief and bright hopes for the future mingled with money to be spent. It was a heady time for all America, not least the furniture industry.

Pent-up demand for consumer goods was unleashed with demobilization. A good portion of young American women had been waiting out the war and planning on marriage soon after. When their boys came home (*if* they came home), they rushed first to the altar and then to the nearest furniture store. Starting around 1945 and continuing well into the 1950s, there was a run on furniture, good, bad, and indifferent. By 1946, American manufacturers had retooled and were already fluent in the new design language. From Grand Rapids to Southern California, furniture called modern started pouring out of the factories, and it could hardly be produced fast enough to satisfy demand.

Once the eager customers got to the store, they were wholly patriotic. The cachet European furniture had held before the war had fallen completely flat. In a victorious postwar frame of mind, Americans were even able to shake off that old, embarrassing inferiority complex. Kowtowing to European culture was replaced with a fierce nationalism, a feeling that if America could win the war, surely it must have something to offer in the field of furniture design. That was coupled with an ardent desire to avoid anything reminiscent of international complications in the living room.

Of foreigners, only the Finn Alvar Aalto, whose bent plywood designs of the late 1930s peaked in popularity after the war, had any immediate success in the American marketplace. In the late '40s, the hot names in quality modern furnishings were Eero Saarinen for Knoll, Edward Wormley for Dunbar of Indiana, T. H. Robsjohn-Gibbings for Widdicomb, and, of course, Charles Eames for Herman Miller. Their success proved that there was a market out there for good design.

WHO IS HERMAN MILLER?

One small manufacturer in particular dared to believe in the existence of a discriminating clientele and made no attempt whatsoever to pander to the "so-called norms of public taste." Instead, from 1945, when it discontinued its line of traditionally trumped-up Sears Roebuck borax, the Herman Miller Furniture Company of Zeeland, Michigan, has been the voice and soul of rational, elegant design in modern residential furniture. Herman Miller bucked "look of the season" hype completely. Its goal, stated in its 1952 catalogue, was a permanent collection of furniture "designed to meet fully the requirements for modern living—not one to be scrapped for each furniture market or for each new trend as announced by the style experts."

COMPREHENSIVE STORAGE SYSTEM/GEORGE NELSON/1959
Systematic storage: a variety of components mounted on aluminum poles gave total flexibility and limitless capacity.

(Photo: Charles Eames)

High principles, indeed, but was it really possible for a small furniture company to make any money that way? For fifteen years or so, it was, and the high-styled creations of Charles Eames, George Nelson, Isamu Noguchi, and Paul Laszlo came off the assembly lines on the flat plains of the Midwest and traveled straight to the heart of sophisticated postwar environments.

But before there was Nelson, before there was Eames, there was D. J. DePree. Son of a tinsmith, he worked for the Michigan Star Furniture Company, then gained control of it in 1919 and renamed it after his father-in-law and business partner, Herman Miller. Not a designer himself, DePree had an uncanny ability to attract top-drawer talent. His first big catch was Gilbert Rohde. In the early '30s, Rohde, a down-on-his-luck young designer who'd just been rejected by every other Grand Rapids-area company he'd visited on a Depression door-knocking tour, convinced DePree, a cheerful, Bible-quoting Calvinist with implacable faith in human nature, to phase out his production of middle-class market staples—reproductions of traditional furniture styles—and to go modern.

The furniture Rohde designed for Herman Miller in the late '30s, though undeniably glamorous, did not sell very well, but that didn't send DePree scurrying back to borax. Instead, it confirmed his belief in functional, unpretentious furniture and in the wisdom of letting brilliant designers do their own unimpeded thing.

When Rohde died in 1944, DePree looked for a new design messiah and found him in the pages of *Life* magazine. Enter George Nelson, a Yale architect, editor of *Architectural Forum*, and a shaping force on the look of America (the indoor shopping mall was his idea, back in 1944). The feature that brought Nelson to DePree's attention was the Storagewall, a 10-inch-wide, fully adjustable, pole-mounted system of stor-

MOLDED PLYWOOD FURNITURE/ CHARLES EAMES/ 1946
The complete collection of molded plywood furniture manufactured by Charles and Ray Eames's own Evans Products Company included dining, card, and coffee tables with steel rod or plywood legs, children's furniture, several variations on the basic chair, and the multifunctional folding screen. When the collection was picked up by Herman Miller in 1947, George Nelson, normally not given to hyperbole, called it "the most advanced furniture being produced in the world today."

age components that immediately rendered such items as armoires, breakfronts, and separate bookcases distinctly "old look."

As design director, George Nelson quickly gathered Charles Eames and sculptor Isamu Noguchi into the Herman Miller family. Nelson was the company's image builder, designing its logo, advertising, graphics, and catalogues. He served as architect for a complex of advanced manufacturing facilities, and he was an eloquent communicator, the spokesperson for a philosophy of rigorous design integrity formulated in the Herman Miller conference rooms. Nelson even offered DePree occasional business advice, such as, "If you can't afford advertising, produce a few products that will get into the magazines because they're odd or crazy."

Odd they may have been to an unenlightened segment of the public, but the furnishings Herman Miller produced through the 1950s—including Eames's plywood group, plastic shell group, lounge with ottoman, and aluminum chair group and Nelson's rosewood and steel-frame case goods lines and comprehensive storage system—were hardly crazy. It was just about the sanest furniture ever produced. That is not to say it was sober or unwhimsical, but above all else, it was rational. Meticulous studies of human anatomy and use patterns of furniture were conducted, and the results suggested the forms Herman Miller furniture would take, down to the smallest angled or curved ramification.

Within three years of Nelson's arrival at Herman Miller, the company had the distinction of producing what was widely recognized as the most advanced furniture in the world, by virtue of its exclusive manufacturing rights to the molded plywood designs of Charles and Ray Eames. These had gained the imprimateur of impeccability in 1946, when they were exhibited by The Museum of Modern Art in its first-ever one-man furniture show. Eames, the luminous talent who is unquestionably America's most important twentieth-century furniture designer, went on to score coup after coup in the late 1940s and '50s for topflight technological and artistic developments in furniture design. The phrase "Eames chair" can mean one of several things: the molded plywood chair whose back is halfway between an oval and a rectangle; the molded fiberglass chair, in all its variations; the luxurious leather and rosewood lounge that has become a status symbol as classic as a Mercedes; or possibly the thin, flat, channel-padded chairs of 1958's aluminum group.

Nor did Eames stop at chairs: his industrial-looking system of storage units, their perforated metal uprights enlivened by Mondrianesque blocks of primary color, and undulating plywood folding screens are testimony to the creative atmosphere that flourished at Herman Miller through the Fifties.

INTERNATIONAL MODERNISM

On the East Coast, another progressive furniture company, today known as Knoll International, had been founded in the early '40s by Hans Knoll, a young man whose father had known Walter Gropius and Miës van der Rohe in Germany and had made furniture for them. Knoll set up a showroom in New York in 1942 and stuck it out through the war years with a new wife, designer Florence Schust of Cranbrook Academy, some designs by the young Danish architect Jens Risom, a supply of discarded army webbing for upholstery, and the novel idea of employing designers on a royalty basis. The concept attracted an illustrious multinational stable, eventually including the Italian Franco Albini, the sculptor in wire Harry Bertoia, the sculptor in steel and stone Isamu Noguchi, Americans Ralph Rapson and George Nakashima, and the Frenchman Pierre Jeanneret. Most significant on the Knoll roster however, was the uninhibited architect Eero Saarinen, whose demanding philosophical inquiries into the nature and meaning of furniture brought forth some of the key pieces of the late 1940s and '50s. Saarinen continued to pursue the truly organic chair, a quest he had begun with Eames in 1940, compromising along the way with the Grasshopper and Womb chairs for Knoll in the late '40s and finally achieving one-piece unity with the pedestal group in 1956.

In the closing moments of the Forties, sparks of new energy ignited in Europe. In Italy, Carlo Mollino, Ico and Luisa Parisi, Marco Zanuso, and others were designing chairs with forms that, besides following function, seemed to be following Art Nouveau and surrealism as well. The Italians were totally unconfined in their flamboyant use of silhouettes and their wild application of jigsaw rhomboids to cabinetry. Their wittiness and drop-dead sophistication made good copy, but precious little of their postwar output found its expensive way to America in the late '40s and early '50s. And so for the time it remained a rarefied taste.

The French, on the other hand, had not regained the luster of their Art Deco heyday. The idea of mass-producing furniture went against their grain. They had grown used to and still appreciated the work of the individual cabinetmaker, or *ébéniste*. Yet, Jean Royère and Jean Prouvé, among others, came to terms with the hand/machine conflict and produced exceptionally stylish, distinctive modern furniture. Though appreciated on its home turf, it did not penetrate the American market to any great degree.

As for the English, the wartime exigency called utility furniture had left its unstylish mark on furniture produced even afterward. Except for the storage units of Robin Day and Clive Latimer, which won first prize in The Museum of Modern Art's 1948 Low-Cost Furniture Design competition, Day's later stacking chairs, and the quirky Antelope chair of Ernest Race, most of

(Photo: Knoll International)

CHAIR/JENS RISOM/1941–42
Danish-American designer Risom used one of the few available wartime materials—surplus army webbing— to create this chair for Hans Knoll. It was gobbled up for use in USO lounges and waiting rooms and was one of Knoll's first successes.

(Photo: The Brooklyn Museum, gift of the Italian government)

(Photo: Fritz Hansen)

TEA TABLE/CARLO MOLLINO/ c. 1950

Carlo Mollino of Turin, Italy, pursued eccentric biomorphic shapes in molded plywood as well as upholstered furniture. This tea table is typical of the bizarre cutout shapes and irregular polygons he liked.

➤ CHAIR/HANS WEGNER/1953

Love of wood is the clear message of this chair for Fritz Hansen, the Copenhagen manufacturer. Grain is paramount, in both the laminated plywood back and seat and solid wood legs.

what was produced in British furniture factories in the late 1940s and '50s and called Contemporary was glum and unexciting.

It was left to the Scandinavians to be the main proponents of International Modernism as we entered the second half of the twentieth century, a role they could ably handle. From Denmark, Sweden, and Finland came furniture artistry of a very high order. The Scandinavian designers made loving, respectful use of an abundant natural resource, wood, and what consumer in the world could feel hesitant about accepting good old natural wood? "Scandinavian modern" was warmer-looking and homier than the American machine-inspired designs. The look won slews of international prizes and soon became one of the most popular design idioms ever to hit the market.

The Scandinavians fared well in the American marketplace for ideological as well as design reasons. The chairs and tables they produced were seen as the tangible expressions of the just, democratic societies that spawned them. Owning a chair by Hans Wegner or Finn Juhl or Alvar Aalto, besides bespeaking good taste, was a peace-loving thing to do.

CHAIRS/CARL JACOBS/1950
Cleverer than ever, furniture did all kinds of new tricks it had never done before. It stacked: manufactured by Kandya in England, these plywood shells, for home and institutional use, had open back cutouts for resiliency and stacking capability.

TURN OF THE MID-CENTURY

What with Herman Miller's runaway success, Knoll bringing out radical new designs every month, mainstream manufacturers like Baker and Widdicomb competing for top-name designers, and the Scandinavian imports rolling in, the look of the American interior was changing.

The transmogrification was helped along by the Good Design shows held biannually from 1950 to 1955 at the industry's major furniture market in Chicago. There selected items were presented to the press and the public after having been given The Museum of Modern Art's stamp of approval.

In California, the Case Study House Program, organized by *Arts and Architecture* magazine, commissioned architects to build experimental modern houses that demonstrated new methods of construction and ways of utilizing and furnishing interior space. A spate of museum exhibitions around the country focusing on furniture-as-functional-art helped educate the public—making them aware of the goods and bads of modern furniture design.

If it is true that trends in interior design tend to mirror changes in the world outside, then homes at mid-century certainly needed changing. Perhaps that world of tomorrow, of which there had been a peek at the 1939 New York World's Fair, had actually arrived.

SOFA COMPACT/CHARLES EAMES/1954

It folded: three flat planes of upholstered foam padding, mounted on
chrome legs, folded compactly for
shipping. The unsensuous sofa was
Eames's sole manufactured attempt at
solving an unpopular design problem.

(Photo: Charles Eames)

CHAIRS/VERNER PANTON/1956

It came apart: Danish designer Panton's
nickel-rod chairs for Fritz Hansen
were completely knockdown, available with suede or poplin slings in
a variety of colors.

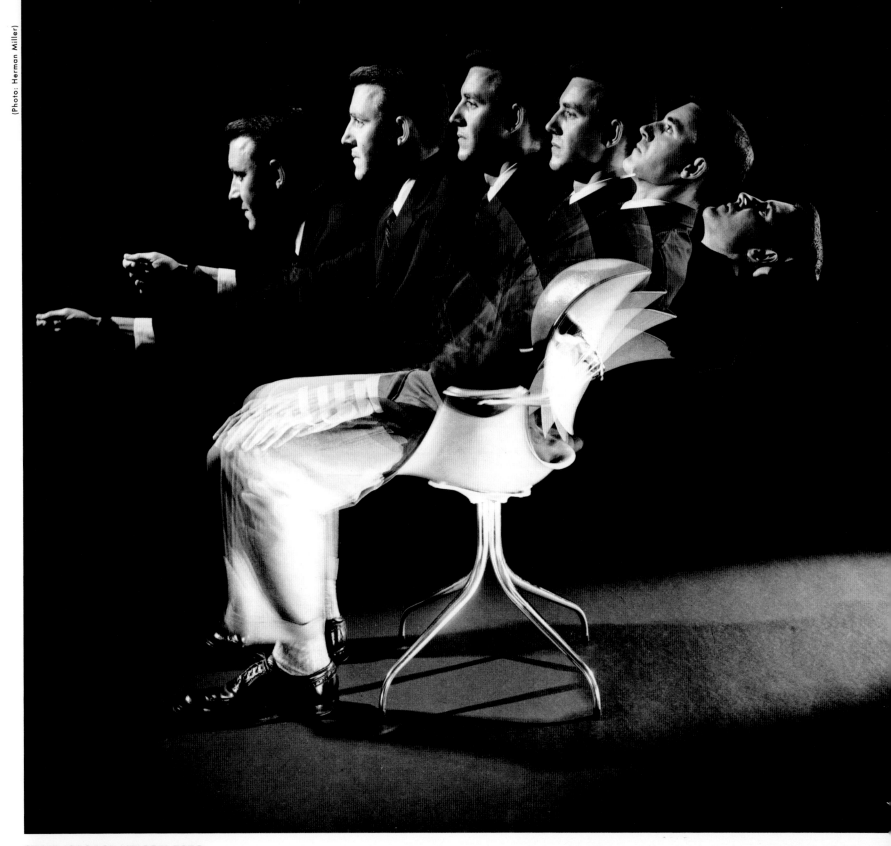

CHAIR/GEORGE NELSON/1958
It flexed: Nelson's swag-legged fiberglass shell for Herman Miller had 90-degree flexibility, as shown in this advertising shot.

(Photo: Vladimir Kagan)

Cranes were everywhere, silhouetted in the sky, as steel-and-glass skyscrapers went up in every metropolis, and bulldozers cleared the way for highways to link them. Jets were shortening international travel times to disorienting briefness. Millions of brand-new television sets filled the air with waves that, when they reached consumers' minds, corrupted them with lust for dream kitchens and extravagantly finned cars like the ones they saw on commercials. The profusion of goods in the stores was matched, in a happy reflection of the postwar economy, by the unprecedented power to buy it and the leisure time to use it.

Cash rich America may have been, but whether the demographic changes of the early '50s really improved the quality of life is open to question. In the name of progress, solidly built Victorian housing stock was abandoned in favor of suburban sprawl. For a quarter-acre of grass and independence, young families traded in the high ceilings, attics, porches, and pantries of their parents' houses. Instead of servants, they had dishwashers and mammoth freezer chests. Instead of many rooms, they had fewer, and the rooms were getting smaller. In a continuation of a trend that had begun during the Depression of the early '30s, builders no longer thought of house proportions in such grandiose terms. Each room was called upon to have more than one function, and so was the furniture in it.

For the first time, factories were manufacturing furnishings that addressed the needs of modern life. "Multipurpose" became a catch phrase. This new furniture stacked, folded, and bent; it was rearrangeable and interchangeable; it nested and flexed. Chairs were designed to be pressed into service for a dozen different reasons. Tables were nonspecific, for eating, writing, or playing cards. The small rooms often had big windows, and furniture scaled long and low to accommodate the new ratio kept appearing, and public taste kept accelerating to embrace it all.

"Casual living" was how the magazines put it—the sort of life-style that necessitated tea carts and croquet sets and lightweight indoor/outdoor furniture that could go from the kidney-shaped pool's patio to in front of the fieldstone fireplace. Luxury gadgets and appliances—toasters, barbecue sets, Mixmasters, bicycles, record albums, skis—created an immediate need for flexible storage systems to keep it all organized and out of sight.

In 1952, George Nelson, recalling the staunch "manifesto quality" of those early attempts at decorating in the modern mode, wrote, "Now the battle is over. . . . Even department stores sell modern furniture. Contemporary design has been around long enough that interior designers no longer feel a burning compulsion to make a public display of their modernity. But this also means that we have something that has been generally accepted as a style, a word which less than a decade back caused serious designers to tear out what was left of their hair. The word was anathema because it was the 'styles' which were being fought. Only now that the smoke has cleared away, we find that we are saddled with exactly what we thought we were fighting . . . [a] style with which we must now cope, whether we like the idea or not. . . ."

PRIME TIME FOR MODERN

Luckily, in the early and mid-'50s, there were enough good designers around, approaching this style from different angles, to keep things from getting boring. The first few years of the decade saw highlights like Harry Bertoia's sculptural winged Diamond chair of stainless-steel wire for Knoll, Danish architect Arne Jacobsen's strange-looking three-legged Ant chair, the Eames molded plastic shells in all their variety of styles and colors, and the elegant chrome-legged leather sling by William Katavolos, Ross Littell, and Douglas Kelley for Laverne.

■Glass and flagstone were major materials in modern domestic architecture of the 1950s. The upholstered furniture is by New York designer Vladimir Kagan.

By then, we had come a long way from the day more than a quarter century earlier when President Hoover had had to decline America's participation in the 1925 Paris Exposition des Arts Décoratifs because, he explained, we *had* no modern decorative art.

Now we not only had it in abundance, but it was enjoying a "fury of public acceptance, undreamt of only a few years ago," according to Alvin Lustig in the 1953 edition of *New Furniture*, an approximately biennial guide to the best of the new furniture production.

Furniture makers in the United States seemed to be out to prove that possibilities in construction technology and materials had by no means been exhausted. Eames, after something of a lull in which he had only perfected and improved his existing designs, was back making furniture history in 1956 with his classic leather-and-rosewood lounge chair, from the time of its introduction the chair of choice of powerful executives and art directors. Saarinen was also hot in '56, both for architectural achievement and for furniture design. He made the cover of *Time* in July for his revolutionary G.M. Center in Warren, Michigan. He did iconoclastic work for Knoll, replacing the typical legs of tables and chairs with aluminum pedestals, spun to look like a stream of paint flowing out of a bucket. Saarinen's pedestal line became ubiquitous space-age symbols, the very idea of a large functional surface being supported by such a slender stem implying that anything was possible.

On the international level, Italy kept up a prodigious flow of industrially produced furniture that nevertheless seemed to lack none of its designers' blithe spirits. Milan was a hotbed of creative energy, its role emphasized by the famous Milan Triennales, a design competition held every third year which attracted the finest furnishings, glass, ceramics, textiles, and metalwork in the civilized world. The influential manufacturer Cesare Cassina brought to bear his standards of technical perfection on the aggressively stylish designs of Giò Ponti (also Italy's foremost modern architect), Carlo de Carli, Gianfranco Frattini, and Ico Parisi. Carlo Mollino of Turin pursued eccentric, biomorphic shapes in molded plywood and upholstered furniture.

Up north, Hans Wegner, Finn Juhl, Poul Kjaerholm, Ilmari Tapiovaara, and scores of other Scandinavian designers continued to champion craft values while humbly acknowledging and cheerfully employing machines for the many operations *they* performed better. The governments of Denmark, Sweden, and Finland took an active interest in supporting the furniture industry, helping maintain high standards and encouraging consumer awareness of good design.

■The "second Renaissance" in Italian furniture design often traded on a deliberately antifunctional appearance, with gravity-defying "floating" parts, spindly wrought-iron curlicues, and the glorification of asymmetry.
(Illustration: Mary Petty from *Homes of the Brave*, T. H. Robsjohn-Gibbings, 1954)

PEDESTAL TABLE/EERO SAARINEN/1956

Optical illusion: Saarinen's pedestal line for Knoll appeared to the Fifties' eye as an extraordinary balancing act—a large surface of marble or Formica supported on a slender stem of strong aluminum.

(Photo: Knoll International)

(Photo: Tim Street-Porter)

■Anonymous entries in the mass-market furniture race. The pink-and-gray color scheme was a Fifties' favorite, ditto the artists' palette motif.

THE PERILS OF PUBLIC TASTE

Under the pressures of popular approval, the modern furniture movement faced its most difficult challenge: maturing gracefully. Wrote Lustig: "Whereas before the enemy was the unbeliever, now it is the superficial devotee—designer, manufacturer, or consumer—who, by unquestioning acceptance of a few shibboleths, makes possible a great wave of mediocrity in the name of design."

While the upper- and upper-middle brows enjoyed the flow of new products and hadn't forgotten their lessons in good design learned at museum shows and in department stores, the opposite element was also enjoying a heyday. Kitsch probably peaked around 1957. That seems to have been the year of the longest cars, the pinkest neon, the greasiest hair, the pointiest shoes. Space/rocket/atomic imagery was everywhere, in chandeliers, wallpaper, clocks, and though it wasn't all bad—witness George Nelson's ball clock for Howard Miller—most of it was.

On October 4, 1957, the age of the satellite arrived. Sputnik beeped its way around the globe, crossing over the United States six times each twenty-four hours. Once again, America's confidence was shaken. Eisenhower held a press conference to assure the nation that Sputnik didn't prove a thing, but it looked as if the competition had gotten serious. The atomic threat loomed large again, and the idea that wars were behind us no longer seemed so certain.

But what did world events (or events above it) have to do with furniture? For one thing, they altered—perceptibly—the buying habits of the general public. A 1957 survey by the *Chicago Tribune* uncovered and identified a new consumer group which "instead of upholding the traditional ideals of thrift and security gives moral sanction to the immediate satisfaction of wants." It quoted a typical young housewife, prime target of the manufacturers, as saying: "I feel I may not live till that rainy day, so I am going to live for each day now." Not exactly the voice of a woman planning to save up for a mahogany highboy, or even an Eames lounge, steeply priced for the time at $430.

It was a pervasive attitude that permitted a general deterioration in the quality of furniture, both in its manufacture and its design. Although some key examples of Fifties iconography were produced in the last three years of the decade, they were not, by and large, American. What has endured from that period are the big "shape" pieces, exaggerated symbols of a decade about to pass into the Pop sensibilities of the Sixties and yield to Italian design supremacy in molded plastics and polyfoam-upholstered modular seating systems.

The Danish architect Arne Jacobsen demonstrated that the sculptural idea of form still had plenty of pep with his hyperbolically rounded Egg and Swan chairs of 1958. Verner Panton, also a Dane, arrived in 1960 at something he'd long been after: a chair of continuous plastic, which followed his 1959 cone-shaped stool/chairs of fabric and wire, their round seats pivoting on a slender point.

In this country, a few good chairs—Norman Cherner's for Plycraft for example and George Nelson's commodious fiberglass shell—did make their way onto the market in the closing years of the decade, but no real landmark pieces were produced.

There had been a brain drain away from the production of residential furniture. Herman Miller was producing mainly contract furnishings for airports, gymnasiums, and corporate offices and leading up to its 1964 introduction of Robert Propst's Action Office, whose explosive success made it financially unnecessary for Herman Miller ever again to make residential furniture of such high quality that it couldn't compete in the flooded market with less expensive imitations.

And as Charles Eames and George Nelson were every bit as fascinated with furniture for industry as they were with furniture for the home, Herman Miller soon stopped dealing with retailers and became purveyor only to corporate clients.

Knoll was another crucial absence from the residential furniture scene. In the late '50s, Florence Knoll was getting her firm's planning unit ever more involved with total solutions to corporate design problems, investing her talents in offices for CBS, conference rooms for Rockefeller, cafeterias for employees of banks and insurance companies.

DESIGN BACKLASH

Fueling the late '50s decline in furniture quality was the refusal of U.S. courts to allow designers to patent their furniture designs. Unscrupulous entrepreneurs turned out copies just a line off the originals and sold them for half the price. Saarinen's pedestal line, on which Knoll had spent thousands in research and development, was seen everywhere in cheaper versions. In a famous case, Sears copied a Lightolier pole lamp and was supported by a judge who ruled that people of low means should be able to afford modern furniture just like anyone else.

Design ideas that had once been introduced at the custom level were being translated into medium-priced, middle-class dialect, with disastrous results. Ornamentation came creeping back where it did not belong, finding its way onto formerly spare and clean-lined pieces. At the 1959 summer market at Chicago's Merchandise Mart, the *New York Times* reported that "straight-lined modern designs are softened, as are all the once-austere modern styles at this market, with caning, inlaid wood, and other ornaments."

The output of many manufacturers began to have a rather strung-out look, either terribly derivative of the originals or surreal and theatrical and in highly suspect

(Photo: The Museum of Modern Art)

TABLE LAMP/JAMES HARVEY CRATE/1950
Early atomic design. This lamp won third prize in The Museum of Modern Art's 1950 lamp design contest. A funnel containing the light source could be directed to reflect on a flat metal disk, connected by three stainless steel rods topped with cork balls.

(Photo: Tim Street-Porter)

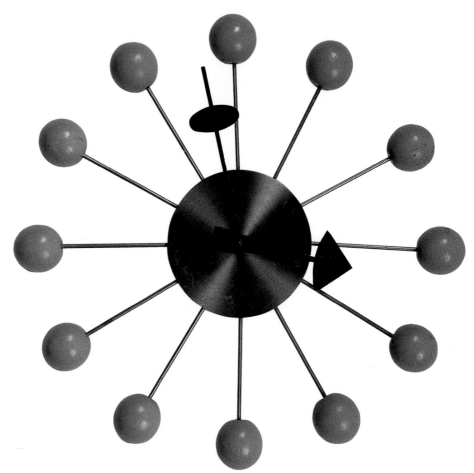

BALL CLOCK/GEORGE NELSON/ 1947
This popular item for the Howard Miller Clock Company had that distinctly atomic age look, like models of molecular structure in chemistry class.

(Photo: Tim Street-Porter)

■A curvaceous coffee table by Ply-craft, a Danish chair, a typically Fifties wire wall sculpture, and one of the most collectible relics of the early electronics age—a Philco Predicta TV.

taste, like the silly furnishings on a Technicolor movie set through which Cyd Charisse was expected to burst momentarily. Some of it was pure Jetsons—most of it bad, some successful, like the clear plastic Tulip and Champagne chairs of Estelle and Erwine Laverne, highly popular and highly imitated.

Worse still, it seemed that the public was not as committed to the concept of modern design as had been previously thought. Interpretations of period styles—Italian Provincial, Rural English, Moorish, Renaissance, Early American, and what have you—flooded the Merchandise Mart at the industry's major trade shows in 1958 and '59.

The bloom was clearly off the rose. Speakers at Chicago denigrated the modern movement, voicing objections to furniture that "flaunted its construction like oil-well rigging." "No amount of structural ingenuity can compensate for the loss of loveliness," said Harvey Probber, a furniture designer. Said architect Edgar Tafel: "We are getting away from the cold modern look, an old-fashioned one today. We like decoration—carving, the use of marble and other materials to enrich the surfaces of a house." Even Paul McCobb, a leading designer of clean-lined case goods for the Winchendon Furniture Company of Massachusetts, was quoted as saying, "The modern revolution is finished and we are all more mature."

Even The Museum of Modern Art, at this time, had apparently given up the ghost. Its Good Design shows had ended abruptly in 1955. At the eleventh Milan Triennale in 1957, there was more interest in glass, ceramics, and silverware than there was in furniture.

THE END OF AN ERA

Mid-Century Modern's golden age was over. If it lasted roughly a decade, its logical borders were 1947 to 1957, not 1950 to 1960.

The actual decade, for furniture design, ended on a rather subdued note. By 1960, it was as if all the innovations of the preceding years had become too much for the public to digest. In large part, it was the cheap copies that rendered the modern furniture movement in America prematurely doomed. A sort of visual fatigue had set in regarding those amazing amorphic shapes and they had simply gone out of vogue. Conservatism prevailed, and what furniture wasn't period reproduction was rigidly squared off, the cult of the right angle seemingly as strong in the early '60s as the free-form curve had been ten years earlier.

Most Scandinavian imports were now "formula" case goods, and the world looked increasingly toward the Italians to provide the creative sparks. Working with

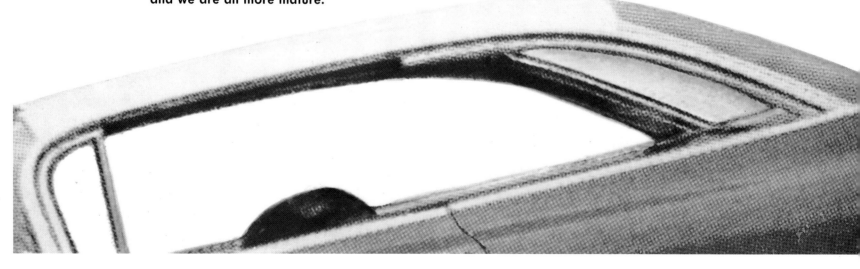

new plastics, designers such as Joe Colombo, Tobia Scarpa, and Gaetano Pesce secured their country's reputation—one it has held onto to this day—as the most venturesome in the world. French and Belgian design got a boost from the 1958 World's Fair in Brussels. Designers Olivier Mourgue and Pierre Paulin seemed to suit the tempo of the new decade, falling right into Pop place with chairs and sofas that, though generously sculptural and brazenly styled, possessed a symmetry the eccentric Fifties never aspired to.

As for America, that lovable, intrepid quality that characterized the best of its Fifties furniture—born of innocence of a computerized world, of minority and youth uprisings, of an intensified nuclear arms race— had fled forever as if on the tail fins of a Cadillac Coupe de Ville. The design climate created by all that high-flying postwar optimism had evaporated.

Along with its bold and daring shapes had gone the last gasp of the unrealistic American dream. Unique and unrepeatable was the spirit of that confident, audacious decade . . . and this book is dedicated to the wonderful furniture it brought forth before its dreams had flown.

(Photo: Herman Miller)

STACKING CHAIR/VERNER PANTON/1960
This fiberglass-reinforced polyester chair brought the postwar quest for unity of form to its logical conclusion. A one-piece continuous chair, it was a visual triumph but tended to crack in use.

BREUER AND BEYOND

(Photo: Tim Street-Porter)

Even the best twentieth-century furniture can only succeed to a point when it is surrounded by the sentimental architecture of the past. It is rare to see a collection of modern furniture in its intended context—in rooms whose proportions suit it, whose plain backdrops set off its sculptural qualities, and where the only ornament is the play of light and shadow through windows so large they have become walls.

This landmark is such a house, one of a very few Marcel Breuer, the Bauhaus-trained architect, designed in America. Built in 1953, it sits on a hill overlooking the Hudson River—long, low, and transparent, except for a few bright planes of primary color. Its interior spaces are warmed by cypress wood ceilings, textural flagstone floors, and the central presence of a white-brick freestanding fireplace.

Such a house needs the right people, and it was fortuitous that, when it was put up for sale by its original owner, Barry Friedman and his wife, Patricia Pastor, bought it; fortuitous because it was the perfect setting for the stockpiles of furniture—all premier examples of mid-century modernism—that Mr. Friedman, an art dealer, had been collecting for years.

Together, the furnishings represent an international overview of significant postwar design. Besides the built-in sofas and cabinets Breuer himself designed, there are French, Italian, and Scandinavian pieces, as well as a great deal of furniture by American masters Eames, Nelson, Saarinen, and Bertoia—all working in complete and effortless harmony and proving that modern furnishings in a modern house can be cheerful, playful, and eminently livable.

■Bruno Mathsson's chairs of bent plywood with webbed upholstery date from 1934, but their exaggerated curves were a clear indication of things to come. The round plywood coffee table is Charles Eames, 1946; a 1947 George Nelson platform bench is used in front of the sofa as another coffee table; and the rug is French, c. 1950.

■An American, Dan Johnson, designed this peculiar chair of metal with a caned seat and back, but it was manufactured in Italy, in the 1950s. The lamp is a table version of Danish designer Poul Henningsen's better-known metal-shaded hanging lamps.

(Photo: Tim Street-Porter)

■Framed in wood and strung with flag line, Jørgen Hovelskov's c. 1957 Harp chair is surprisingly sittable. The standing lamp is French, 1950s.

(Photo: Tim Street-Porter)

■Breuer's design for a built-in sofa includes a lighted shadow box behind for display of *objets*.

■The Nelson home/office desk of 1946 was an unfamiliar form when first presented, but its conscientious planning convinced skeptics. A leather-covered surface folds out to reveal typewriter space; the metal perforated drawer on the right holds files; a rectangular cabinet with sliding doors keeps clutter at hand but out of sight. The swivel chair on casters is Arne Jacobsen's; the side table, by Jens Risom; and the rug, unexpectedly, Chinese, made in the 1950s for export to the Western world.

■By its airplane-wing silhouette and thick-and-thin modeling of wood, this Italian tea cart is very much a product of its age: the 1950s.

■The gateleg dining table by Swedish designer Bruno Mathsson dates from the 1940s. Complementing it magnificently are blond wood chairs by Joe Atkinson for American maker Thonet, 1952. Overhead hangs Henningsen's PH-5 lamp. The long wall-mounted cabinet is Breuer's own, remarkably similar to those in his 1930s houses.

(Photo: Tim Street-Porter)

(Photo: Tim Street-Porter)

■Nelson's thin-edge beds for Herman Miller, accompanied by his swagged-leg side table, are used in the master bedroom.

■The sculptural qualities of George Nelson's 1958 swagged-leg fiberglass shell chair are illuminated by a cantilevered French floor lamp of metal with a plastic shade.

■The chair, part of Saarinen's 1948 collection for Knoll, was intended primarily for institutional use. The low wire-base table is Noguchi for Knoll, c. 1954; the rug and lamp are both French.

■The most outrageous of the 1946 Eames molded plywood chairs is the variation clad in pony skin.

■Nesting tables of bent plywood with a silken finish are by Danish designer Greta Jalk, 1959.

COCONUT CHAIR/GEORGE NELSON/1957
A comfortable triangle of a chair, resting on three legs atop a European rug.

(Photo: Tim Street-Porter)

(Photo: Tim Street-Porter)

■A 1952 desk by French designer Jean Prouvé is teamed with an exuberant American chair by Norman Cherner for Plycraft, 1956.

■An ultrastylish desk with a free-form top in Formica; leather-covered drawers below. The designer is unknown. The fiberglass chair with its generously cutout back is by E. & E. Laverne, 1958; the lamp, by leading French lighting designer Serge Mouille. Even the phone is design conscious, made by Ericka of Sweden.

(Photo: Tim Street-Porter)

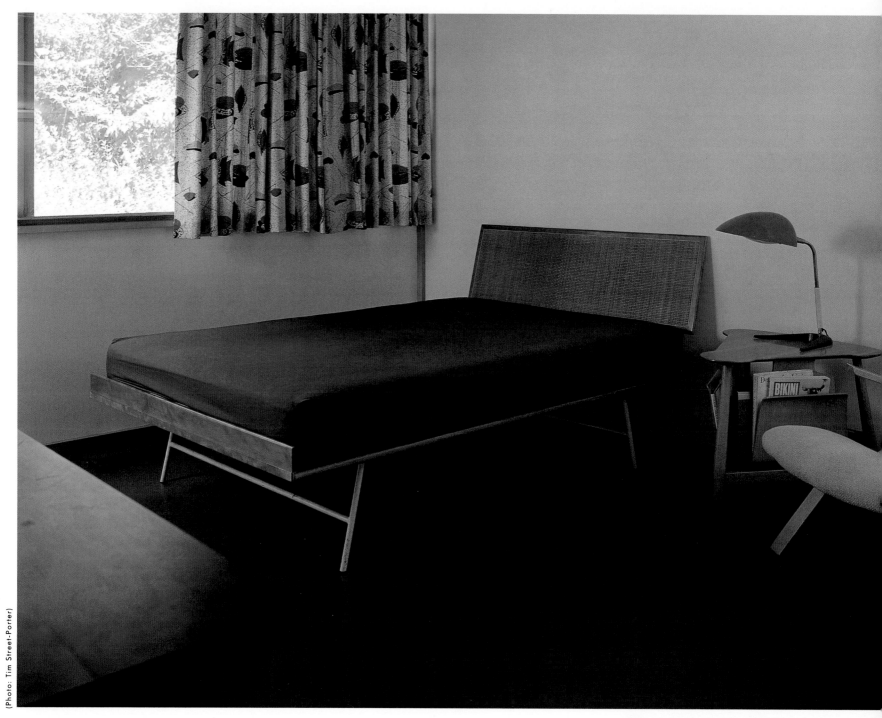

■The guest bedroom features Nelson's
thin-edge bed for Herman Miller.

■The guest house, reached via a wide covered stairway,
is furnished with tilting Bird chairs by Harry Bertoia, tall-
back companions to the more common Diamond chairs,
all 1952. The wall cabinets are Breuer built-ins; the
Formica-and-wood coffee table by Californian Paul
Laszlo; the geometric rug is French; and the metal screen
of unknown origin.

(Photo: Tim Street-Porter)

■The capsule-shaped couch and chairs are of woven fiber with wrought-iron legs, designer anonymous; ditto the nesting cocktail tables of painted wood and metal.

■A French designer named Hoffer borrowed the spider's idea for these patio chairs. They fold completely flat for portability and storage. Mid-1950s.

THE LOOKS

Like it or not, George Nelson suggested in 1953, a style is what we have. Modern was an identifiable style, to be sure. Although a well-oiled Danish chair had little in common with one in wire mesh, even an unpracticed eye had no trouble correctly tagging each of them with the Modern label—but its exact definition left people bemused.

Mid-Century Modern furniture had no single hallmark. There was no egg-and-dart molding to shout Greek Revival, no convenient pediment to signify Chippendale. Its identity was based on the very absence of ornament and on the new materials and silhouettes.

During the postwar decade, three dominant "looks" emerged within the modern category. Nelson called them the biomorphic look, the machine look, and the handcrafted look. It is a rare piece of Mid-Century Modern furniture that does not display one of these influences to some degree.

▶ **VASE/ALVAR AALTO/1937**
Early free-form. The glorious asymmetry that was possible before the war only in molten glass was possible after the war in furniture.
(Photo: The Museum of Modern Art)

(Photo: Herman Miller)

THE BIOMORPHIC LOOK

Most obviously Fifties and perhaps most fun in retrospect is furniture with biomorphic tendencies (dictionary defined as "evoking images of biological organisms without representing any specific organisms"). Thanks to new materials and technologies, the plastic, free-form qualities of protoplasm could be achieved in three dimensions and made solid.

The asymmetry of the biomorphic look was an appealing novelty after centuries of furniture whose two halves had always mirrored each other. The amoeba became the darling of graphic artists, potters, and neon sign makers. Then, of course, the one-celled creature was gobbled up by the furniture industry and its fluid profile was regurgitated in the form of millions of unsubtle coffee tables, becoming a tiresome sight by the end of the decade. But the abuse of the biomorphic concept in no way detracted from the contributions of the high practitioners of the look.

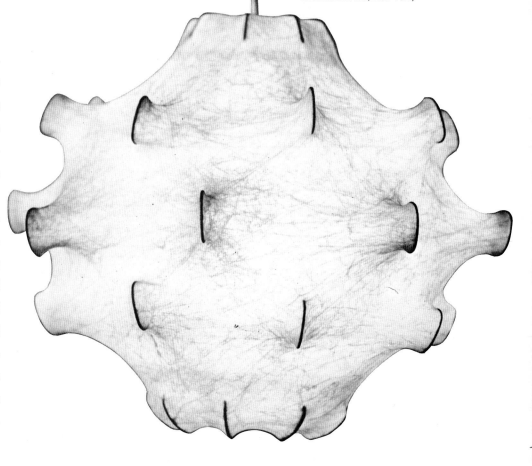

TARAXACUM LAMP/A. & P. C. CASTIGLIONI/1950
To know this lamp is to touch it: its spun fiberglass "skin" feels eerily human.
(Photo: Philadelphia Museum of Art/Atelier International Ltd., New York)

TABLE/ISAMU NOGUCHI/late 1940s
A highly individualistic table of ebonized plywood, designed for Herman Miller but deemed too quirky to be mass-produced.

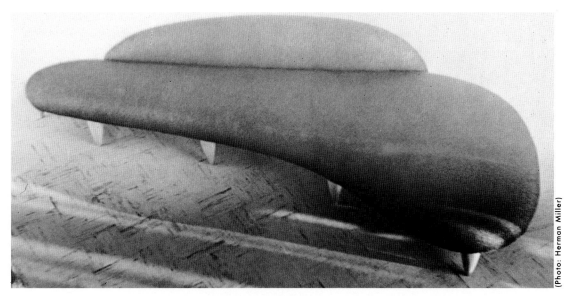

SOFA/ISAMU NOGUCHI/late 1940s
The same fate met this dramatically uneven sofa on little blond conical legs—never produced.

(Photo: Herman Miller)

CHAISE LONGUE/CHARLES EAMES/ 1948

An Eames experiment for the purely sculptural joy of it, the whimsical off-center lounge never had its sittability tested to the full. A thin plastic "sandwich" outer shell was filled with vermiculite, a wonder mineral that expands with heating for rigidity and strength.

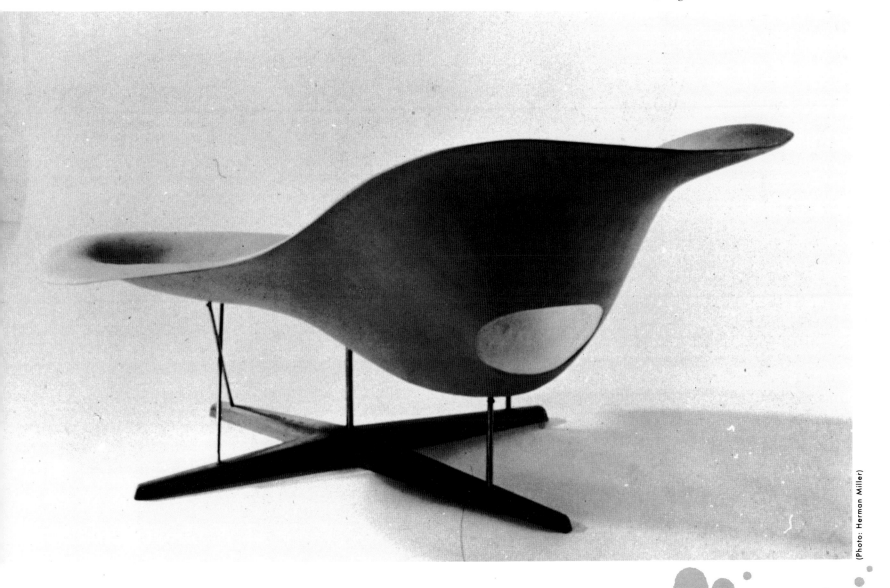

(Photo: Herman Miller)

SOFA & COFFEE TABLE/VLADIMIR KAGAN/c. 1952

Sofa for seven: Kagan, still in his twenties, masterfully rendered biomorphic shapes in spring-foam upholstered pieces. The free-form glass tabletop echoes the theme, while the sculptured walnut base suggests an Italian influence.

THE MACHINE LOOK

Diametrically opposite furniture inspired by living tissue was the hard machine look, an echo of the 1930s "let's celebrate the role of the machine" battle cry. After World War II, the hand versus machine conflicts that had so torn furniture designers in the first three decades of the century and produced a splintering of movements—de Stijl, Constructivism, Bauhaus—each with its own idea of appropriate furniture for the machine age, had largely abated. The virtue of furniture made by machine was no longer subject to anybody's impugning.

In the Fifties, the art lay in not being overly artful about the machine. While the polished tubular steel furniture of the Bauhaus always had undeniable elegance, the wire-strut base of an Eames chair or perforated-metal elements of an Eames storage unit were something quite different—much franker in their admission of functionality and technical nitty-gritty.

A lot of furniture designed by architects fell into the machine category. In the vast cubic spaces of many a modern house, factory-style furniture made consummate sense.

(Photo: Wendell Lovett)

FLEXI-FIBRE CHAIR/WENDELL H. LOVETT/1952
The wire-rod base construction of this fiber-covered plastic chair is unapologetically high-tech.

T CHAIR/WILLIAM KATAVOLOS, ROSS LITTELL & DOUGLAS KELLEY/c. 1952
A dichotomy of textures and temperatures: leather sling seat on chrome-plated and black-enameled steel frame base.

(Photos: Mark Meacham/The Liliane Stewart Collection, Le Château Dufresne, Musée des Arts Décoratifs de Montréal)

➤ **CHAIRS/POUL KJAERHOLM/1955**
A new slant on International Style
furniture—Kjaerholm's range of chairs
for Fritz Hansen in flat steel, their
coldness offset by cane upholstery.

THE HANDCRAFTED LOOK

In a bizarre twist on the pure ideals of a William Morris or a Gustav Stickley, who viewed handcrafted values as the salvation of a world gone machine-mad, a third most popular furniture fashion of the 1950s was the handcrafted look, which was often achieved with considerable help from power tools and assembly operations.

Most successful at blending the two poles were Scandinavian designers such as Hans Wegner, Finn Juhl, and Ilmari Tapiovaara. Not one iota of the comforting, homey quality of their light wood furniture was ever sacrificed to manufacturing considerations.

Of the three expressions, the handcrafted look was most acceptable to the general public. It was easier to understand than either the avant-garde biomorphic approach or the machine look, which many claimed to find cold and clinical. The result was an explosion of interest in what was commonly called, sometimes accurately, Danish Modern.

CHAIR/K. & E. CLEMMENSEN/1958
Good from afar and even better up close, this strapping chair combines tight-fitting leather upholstery with delicate modeling of wood.

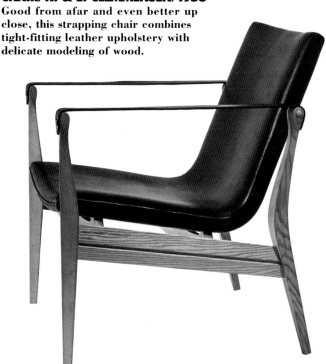

(Photo: Fritz Hansen)

▶ **THREE-LEGGED CHAIR/HANS WEGNER/c. 1949**
A superb specimen of Scandinavian craft integrity, a variation on the classic known simply as "the chair." Gracefully tapered legs, a back rail that segues into an armrest, and a rope, rush, or ply seat. What more is needed?

(Photo: Fritz Hansen)

THE TEN BEST MID-CENTURY CHAIRS: FORM, FUNCTION, AND FLAMBOYANCE

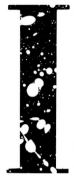n theory, one can sit on almost anything, including the floor. In practice, citizens of the twentieth century have been extremely picky about what they do sit on.

As George Nelson pointed out in his 1953 book, *Chairs*, every culture seems to focus its decorative arts efforts on a particular symbolic item. For the ancient Egyptians, it was the sarcophagus. In the post–World War II Western world, the exalted object was the chair.

The chair played a starring role in rooms of the late 1940s and '50s, with very little competition. In the modern house, the chair came by its status as a result of attrition. Most of the other furniture had disappeared, either literally or visually. Built-in sofas, storage walls, recessed lighting, and general spareness were the rule. The walls were often made of glass and, therefore, vanished, leaving furniture without a backdrop and creating a need for chairs that looked good from any angle. In this minimized interior landscape, chairs became more important than ever.

Mid-century furniture designers loved the chair. It challenged them intellectually, gratified them aesthetically, and made them famous. Certainly no other piece of furniture was as good for their imaginations. And no other furniture was given such wonderful, affectionate nicknames—the Grasshopper, the Womb, the Egg, the Ant, the Swan, the Sling, the Tulip, the Lady, the Antelope, the Coconut. These were chairs to make people smile. Their shapes were bold, even outrageous, and they entered into popular iconography via the cover of the *Saturday Evening Post* (Saarinen's Womb) and ads for Coca-Cola (Santa in an Eames chair).

Mid-century chairs were more comfortable than their Bauhaus predecessors, designed, as they often were,

"Sitting is basically a human invention—a compromise between standing up and lying down."

HANS WEGNER

ANT CHAIR/ARNE JACOBSEN/1953
The narrow back of this light, sturdy, stackable design oddity is for flexibility as well as visual interest. Beech, teak, oak, and maple were among the nine layers of plywood heated and molded into subtle but complex curves. A number of similar designs by Jacobsen were produced by Copenhagen manufacturer Fritz Hansen in the early and mid-'50s—all interesting shapes, but the Ant chair remains the most special.
(Photo: Fritz Hansen)

◢ MOLDED PLASTIC SHELL CHAIR/ CHARLES EAMES/1950

A phenomenally serviceable chair made of fiberglass and resin, a material used for crash helmets. You could roll this chair down a mountain and hardly damage it. First developed in metal, it won second prize in The Museum of Modern Art's 1948 Low-Cost Furniture Design competition. For manufacture two years later, metal was replaced by a sturdier plastic. In six original Fifties fashion colors: greige, elephant-hide gray, lemon yellow, seafoam green, parchment, and red, and a choice of bases.

(Photo: Herman Miller)

◢ TECNO CHAIR/OSWALDO BORSANI/ 1955

Gifted offspring of the marriage between Borsani and Tecno of Milan, this wonderful lounge is almost architectural in scope, so imposing is its presence. You name it, it adjusts—the back, the footrest, the angle of the seat—by fractions of an inch on smooth gears within its neatly upholstered, firm body. Even the armrests arch either up or down.

(Photo: Tim Street-Porter)

DIAMOND CHAIR/HARRY BERTOIA/ 1952

A chair made up mostly of light and air, corraled by a grid of chrome-plated stainless-steel wire, the spread-eagled Diamond chair is one of Knoll's all-time successful designs. It has been made continuously since 1950 in exactly the same way—surprisingly, by hand, in a wooden apparatus for bending the wire which proved more practical and less expensive than bending it by machine. One version tilted on its axis. A tall-backed vari- ation was also available. Armless versions in plastic-coated wire or molded plastic are familiar sights in the atriums of public buildings and company cafeterias. Bertoia worked with Eames in the early '40s, experiment- ing with plywood, and realized his own preference for working in metal. "It was my nature," he said, "to take a rod and bend it."

(Photo: Philadelphia Museum of Art)

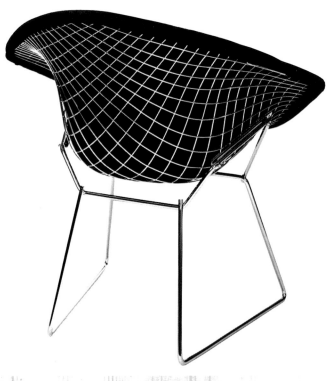

SLING CHAIR/JORGE FERRARI- HARDOY/1938

This chair has the whiff of scandal about it, subject of copyright infringe- ment lawsuits by the dozen. It was de- signed before the war by a group of Argentinian architects, and they bor- rowed the idea from a folding wooden British officer's chair of the nineteenth century. The Sling, Butterfly, or Hardoy chair has been knocked off to the tune of about 5 million copies, the legitimate version made in the post- war years by Knoll.

(Photo: Knoll International)

for the newly acceptable activity known as lounging. They were concerned with the human spine in an anthropomorphic way that their elegant ancestors—Miës van der Rohe's Barcelona chair, Breuer's Wassily, even Corbu's Grand Confort—were not.

The mid-century chair's biggest break with the past was the completely separate treatment of base and seat. Before 1940, the legs of a chair generally flowed visually into the horizontal portion and were made of the same material. That year, in The Museum of Modern Art's Organic Design in Home Furnishings competition, Eames and Saarinen showed the world that seating units could be totally independent—in design and execution—of their supporting substructure. It allowed a new playfulness in a chair's construction, new freedom in its silhouette, and it ushered in the age of mix-and-match chair parts. Eames's fiberglass shell, for example, was available at various times with steel rod legs, wooden dowel legs, a wire cage base, a wire "Eiffel Tower" base, a cast-aluminum base, and birch rockers.

In materials, the story of the chair is almost the whole story. Chairs of the postwar decade chronicle the evolution of materials technology, from the delights of molded plywood in the late '40s to the vogue for black wrought iron in the mid-'50s, from the impeccable woodworking of the Scandinavians to the barrage of synthetics out of the industrial labs.

Picking just ten chairs to highlight out of the profusion of great mid-century chairs is no easy task. In informal surveys of experts and aficionados, no two lists ever coincide. The only answer seems to be to present this list in the spirit in which the chairs themselves were conceived: in fun. It is not a definitive ten best by any means, but a selection of chairs significant for bold iconography, radical technical advances, and proven design endurance. With the exception of the Coconut chair, all are still being manufactured today.

"A chair should not only look well as a piece of sculpture in a room when no one is in it, it should also be a flattering background when someone is in it."

EERO SAARINEN

▲ WOMB CHAIR, SOFA, AND OTTOMAN/EERO SAARINEN/1948

The Womb chair was conceived when Florence Knoll told Eero Saarinen she was "sick of those chairs that hold you in one position." Executed in molded fiberglass padded with foam upholstery, its wide, flaring contours encouraged slouching and sprawling and were perfect for the casual body language of the Fifties. The public picked right up on the Womb as a symbol of those crazy things modern furniture designers were doing, and it entered popular iconography via ads, cartoons, and magazine covers. Extended, it became a couch.

(Photo: Knoll International)

◢ PEDESTAL CHAIR COLLECTION/EERO SAARINEN/1956

Sci-fi movies of the day must have used them, so advanced did Saarinen's pedestal line for Knoll look at the time of its introduction. Of his fluid, curvaceous furniture, Saarinen said, "The undercarriage of chairs and tables makes an ugly, confusing, unrestful world. I wanted to clean up the slum of legs and make the chair all one thing again." That had been Saarinen's quest since the 1940 Museum of Modern Art Organic Design contest, and in 1956 it happened, visually at least. The pedestal itself was actually made of metal and joined to the plastic-coated fiberglass seating shell.

(Photo: Knoll International)

◢ MOLDED PLYWOOD CHAIRS/ CHARLES EAMES/1946

The contours of its back and seat are ambiguous round-cornered rectangles, but how well, for a small chair, it stands alone. These are not two-by-two chairs in need of lamps and tables to define their presence within a room. Yet they are unassuming—Eames liked furniture to take a back seat to its surroundings and discarded hundreds of preliminary sketches in an effort to tone down any jet-age, ready-for-take-off character. The five-ply birch or walnut plywood chairs came high, low, padded, painted, even pony-skin-covered. Legs were thick lengths of molded, laminated plywood or steel rods attached via rubber mounts.

George Nelson said it all when he called this the "outstanding chair design of the past two decades . . . a completely integrated expression of form, function, and manufacture."

(Photo: The Brooklyn Museum)
(Photo: Herman Miller)

(Photo: Tim Street-Porter)

EGG CHAIR/ARNE JACOBSEN/1958

Whosoever has swiveled in an Egg chair knows the meaning of all-enveloping. While it is comfortable, it is also a powerful chair, bestowing an aura of instant importance on the sitter. Hence its popularity in corporate conference rooms. Jacobsen, a Danish architect, designed the furniture for many of his commissions, as well as textiles and appliances. Two of his major chairs—the Egg and the Swan—were part of Jacobsen's design package for the Royal Hotel in Copenhagen. For Fritz Hansen, the maker of the Egg chair, the problem lay in fitting the fabric or leather upholstery snugly to the foam padding over a plastic shell.

COCONUT CHAIR/GEORGE NELSON/ 1957

A distinctive wedge of a chair, and no quarrels with comfort. The Coconut's all-of-a-piece seat, back, and arms certainly achieved the old ideal of visual unity. Sprung from the design office of Nelson Associates and manufactured by Herman Miller.

(Photo: Herman Miller)

"The chair remains unassimilable and in consequence it becomes very conspicuous . . . as much a piece of sculpture as an object of utility. The once-humble chair has emerged as a thoroughly glamorous object." GEORGE NELSON

THE DESIGNERS: THE AMERICANS

he most interesting American furniture of the 1950s—the bench-mark designs of such visionaries as Charles Eames and Eero Saarinen, which today constitute the most memorable output of the entire period—at the time represented only 5 percent of all furniture sold.

More accessible psychologically to the general public were the distinguished, urbane, light wooden cabinets and low armchairs of such designers as T. H. Robsjohn-Gibbings, Edward Wormley, and Paul McCobb. Produced by Widdicomb, Dunbar, and Winchendon, respectively, these were of high quality and were as sedulously imitated as the most outrageous shapes of the avant-garde designers.

Although furniture manufacturing was decentralized throughout the country, a high proportion came out of the traditional center, the Grand Rapids, Michigan, area. Sales of modern furniture were at first concentrated in the Northeastern havens of sophistication, but as California grew in the 1950s, modern furniture had quick, widespread success there. In 1957, furniture sales in California topped those of New York for the first time.

Californian contributions to the good design movement were substantial, from the hallowed name of Eames to Paul Laszlo, Paul Tuttle, Kipp Stuart, Stewart MacDougall, Milo Baughman, and the designing/retailing team of Henrik Van Keppel and Taylor Green.

In addition to the popularity of mass-manufactured goods in California and the New York area, custom clienteles supported their favorite designers, bringing into existence many one-of-a-kind pieces, interesting not only for their rarity but for the striking nonconformity of their designs.

"I think of myself officially as an architect. I can't help but look at the problems around us as problems of structure—and structure is architecture."

CHARLES EAMES

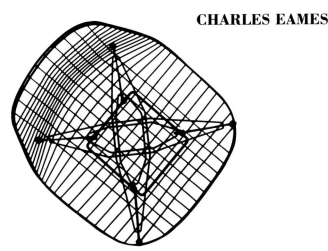

■Three shining lights of Herman Miller together in one shot: central is Noguchi's free-form table with its massive parabolic leg and similar stools, the sunken vase certainly a novel idea. Shown too are Eames's plywood screen and Nelson's cabinet and clock.

CHARLES AND RAY EAMES

Charles Eames is the undisputed shining light of twentieth-century American furniture design. Ray Kaiser Eames, his wife and collaborator, has been cast somewhat in shadow. Not that she ever minded: "Charles was a genius," she says. "I could never have done it myself." Though neither, perhaps, could he. The two worked side by side from 1940 until his death in 1978, from the early days of the plywood molding experiments through the last design for Herman Miller—a sofa that was not put into production until 1984.

The starting point of many of their designs was, more often than not, a friend's voicing a need for a particular piece of furniture. "That's the way things usually happened," Ray Eames recalled. "Someone would be having a baby and needed a rocking chair, so we would design one. The aluminum group came about as a result of a friend's request for indoor/outdoor furniture. There was never a chance to think, what shall we do next? One thing led to another—there was always something that needed doing, a hole that needed filling."

From the needs of the few came furniture for the many. The Eameses' end view was always to create a product that could be mass-produced with ease. Says Ray Eames: "We wanted to get as much quality as possible into mass production so that more people could live with well-made things."

The products of their philosophy—furniture wrought of heavy-duty materials such as aluminum-polyester resin, reinforced with fiberglass, and, of course, plywood, and approached with an architect's concern for structure and spatial relations—had extraordinary impact not only on the look of the mid-century but on the decades beyond.

CHARLES (1907–1978) AND RAY EAMES
Between them, the Eameses were architects, furniture designers, filmmakers, graphic artists, and toy makers. He is the unexcelled creative genius of American modern furniture design, she the indispensable collaborator. "My role was never defined," says Ray Eames, "I just did everything I could do."

CHILDREN'S CHAIRS/CHARLES EAMES/1943
Of laminated birch in red, blue, black, pink, or yellow, these products of Eames's early experiments in molding plywood showed that his furniture had the potential to be downright charming.

(Photo: Herman Miller)

STORAGE UNIT/CHARLES EAMES/1951
WIRE CHAIRS/CHARLES EAMES/1951

Lightweight and lighthearted, the entirely customizable Eames Storage Units resemble the steel-framed house Charles and Ray Eames designed for themselves in 1948 to prove it was possible to construct an inexpensive, livable house out of standard, factory-available parts. Three years later, the Storage Units became the furniture extension of the concept, utilizing perforated aluminum, dimpled plywood, and masonite panels in clear, nonvoguish colors. Shown here with the wire shell chairs of 1951.

(Photo: Tim Street-Porter/Fifty/50, New York)

EXPERIMENTAL CHAIR/CHARLES EAMES/c. 1944

A rarely seen picture of a never-produced design: a molded plywood chair with round seat and long, projecting rear leg. The rubber shock mounts joining wood to steel did, however, survive in other chairs.

PLYWOOD FURNITURE GROUPING/ CHARLES EAMES/c. 1945

Arranged and photographed by Eames to show his latest creations off to advantage. This early collection was manufactured by the Evans Products Company of Venice, California.

**ELLIPSE TABLE/
CHARLES EAMES/
1950
SHELL CHAIRS/
CHARLES EAMES/
1950**
The black laminate surfboard-shaped table, mounted on wire-strut bases, is almost Zen in its simplicity. Placement of the bases varied from angled to straight, centered or near the edge. Seafoam-green fiberglass chairs on low wire-strut bases are a particularly pleasing rendition of their type.

**WIRE CHAIRS/CHARLES EAMES/
1952
TABLE/CHARLES EAMES/1950s**
Pushing it a bit, perhaps, but in 1957
Herman Miller ran this ad to make
the point that Eames furniture was not
only functional, it could be glamorous, too.

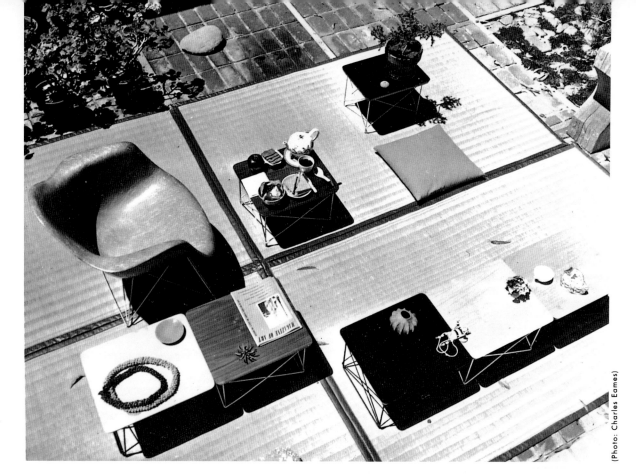

FIBERGLASS SHELL CHAIR AND LOW TABLES/CHARLES EAMES/1951
Pure and simple: Eames photographed this patio setting featuring his wire-based tables using overhead angles and deep shadows to create drama around one of his most rudimentary designs.

(Photo: Charles Eames)

OFFICE SETTING/CHARLES EAMES/ 1949
The Erector Set office: myriad variations on a few basic components out of few materials—plywood, fiberglass, perforated aluminum, and wire—had repercussions later on much more sophisticated office systems.

(Photo: Charles Eames)

(Photo: Herman Miller)

◢ LOUNGE CHAIR AND OTTOMAN/ CHARLES EAMES/1956

Definitely a masculine chair in men's club tradition, with all the weight and sobriety the image implies. Call its frank construction ungainly—huge leather cushions joined to three rosewood shells, mounted on a cast-aluminum, five-pronged base—but the rosewood lounge was and is a quintessential status symbol, additionally popular because its comfort cannot be denied.

◢ SIDE CHAIR/CHARLES EAMES/1958

Most successful aesthetically of the aluminum group was the version without arms to break up its thin, channel-padded profile.

(Photo: Herman Miller)

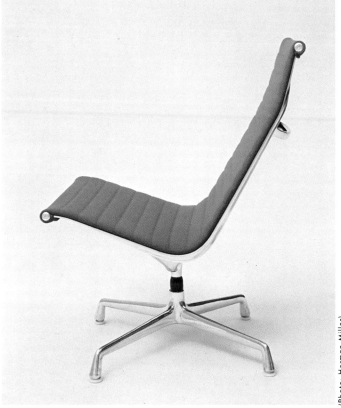

(Photo: Herman Miller)

◢ ALUMINUM GROUP/CHARLES EAMES/1958

The aluminum-ribbed chairs were a decisive step in Eames's turning his interests from the home to the institutional sphere. There were swiveling side chairs on a pedestal base of die-cast aluminum, with high, low, arm, and armless variations, and an executive lounge that reclined, tilted, and swiveled. Usually upholstered in Naugahyde.

■Strong graphics in these early Fifties ads for Herman Miller emphasized the seminal shapes of the furniture—the lines, curves, and complex grid that were the basis of the Eames fiberglass shell and wire chair.

GEORGE NELSON

An architect can't bear to see a promising interior cluttered up with a lot of unrelated, superfluous possessions. Perhaps that is why, throughout his career at Herman Miller, George Nelson was intensely concerned with storage problems—objects management. In the late 1940s, he invented the Storagewall, a flexible system of case pieces mounted on aluminum poles to assuage the pet peeve of the home front: lack of closet space.

Next came the Basic Cabinet Series, introduced in 1947, with rectilinear components arrayed on supporting benches. After a decade of refinements, the BCS involved more complex units, which were available in four finishes (tawny walnut, comb-grain oak, bittersweet red, and gunmetal), with satin chrome or porcelain pulls, and triangular aluminum or 7-inch legs.

(Photo: Herman Miller)

GEORGE NELSON (b. 1908)

As design director for Herman Miller from 1945 through the early '60s, Nelson built its corporate image more successfully than his own. He is nonetheless a Renaissance man—architect, furniture designer, exhibit designer, writer, graphic artist, and teacher. Some critics consider him the most influential design figure of the period.

(Photo: Herman Miller)

CABINETS/GEORGE NELSON/1950s

Little aluminum legs and "satin chrome" pulls add pizzazz to this group; the separate cabinet sections are clearly visible.

PLATFORM BENCH/GEORGE NELSON/1947

As spare as a Haiku and as perfectly formed, this was the basic building block of early Nelson case goods. It had obvious multipurpose intentions and succeeded as coffee table or bench, too.

(Photo: Herman Miller)

CABINETS/GEORGE NELSON/ c. 1947

The media center of the late '40s—audio and video in one long low unit, with a blonde finish to match the on-screen hairdos.

(Photo: Herman Miller)

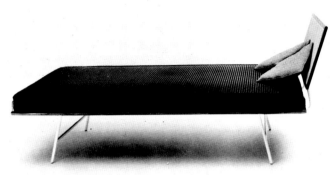

*This versatile platform bench
by George Nelson can serve
as a table, as a base for one
storage cabinet, as a bench
or a plant rest. Truly a
multi-purpose piece.
Available in six lengths—
48" to 102"—and two finishes—
primavera with ebonized base
or all-ebonized.
Professional discounts, of course.*

herman ⋃ iller, zeeland, michi

showrooms—one park avenue, new yo

merchandise mart, chicago 54

exhibitors' building, grand rapids

8810 beverly blvd., los angeles

PLATFORM BENCH/GEORGE NELSON/1947
A self-explanatory advertisement with typically strong graphic
impact from Herman Miller.

BED/GEORGE NELSON/1950s
Nelson's thin-edge beds had a true-to-period profile.
Upholstered foam slabs, they reduced the subject to lean-
est essentials and ended up elegant.

MARSHMALLOW SOFA/GEORGE NELSON/1956

A unique seating piece, to say the least, by George Nelson Associates for Herman Miller. Circular leather or Naugahyde-covered foam disks, as resilient as their candy counter-parts, were at-tached with special chrome-plated connectors to a supporting steel frame. Orange, pink, and purple was a favorite color combo. In production from 1956 to 1965, only a few hun-dred were ever made. This is the 1956 prototype.

(Photo: Mark Meachem, The Liliane Stewart Collection, Le Château Dufresne, Musée des Arts Décoratifs de Montréal, gift of the designer)

CABINET/GEORGE NELSON/1950s

The thin-edge rosewood group was the late-'50s extension of the Basic Cabi-net Series concept, but in its slickness some of the beauty was gone.

(Photo: Herman Miller)

SIDE CHAIR/GEORGE NELSON/1946

Foam slabs on a tubular steel frame made a fashionable chair in the '40s. Nelson's had a back attractive enough to be viewed through the glass walls of a modern house.

(Photo: Herman Miller)

DINING ROOM/GEORGE NELSON/ 1950s

Two of Nelson's most popular residential furniture lines are combined in this Herman Miller catalog shot: The swag-legged dining table and chairs and the rosewood group of infinitely interchangeable case pieces.

SECTIONAL CHAISE/GEORGE NELSON/1955

A new frontier in furniture flexibility. Take a broad, well-upholstered chair and a matching ottoman. Clip on an arm or two and a round table for a drink at one's elbow. *Voilà!*

(Photo: Herman Miller)

(Photo: Herman Miller)

LIVING ROOM/GEORGE NELSON/1958
An all-Nelson living room, with Coconut chairs and rosewood group furniture.

Nelson obviously enjoyed the chal-
lenges of clock design and took
advantage of the opportunity to break
away from the rectangular shapes of
his case goods and produce some of the
most outrageously shaped timepieces
of the era.

(Photo: Tim Street-Porter)

(Photo: Tim Street-Porter)

(Photo: Herman Miller)

KANGAROO CHAIR/GEORGE NELSON/1956
This man-sized club chair scored points for comfort but was not an aesthetic success.

VLADIMIR KAGAN

The great shapes of Kagan are few of a kind. Designer to Manhattan's East Side custom trade, Kagan brought together two popular Fifties approaches: liberal use of extravagant biomorphic shapes and refreshing respect for wood in solid—not plied—form. The nubbly neutral textiles adding character to Kagan's designs are by his longtime partner, Henry Dreyfuss.

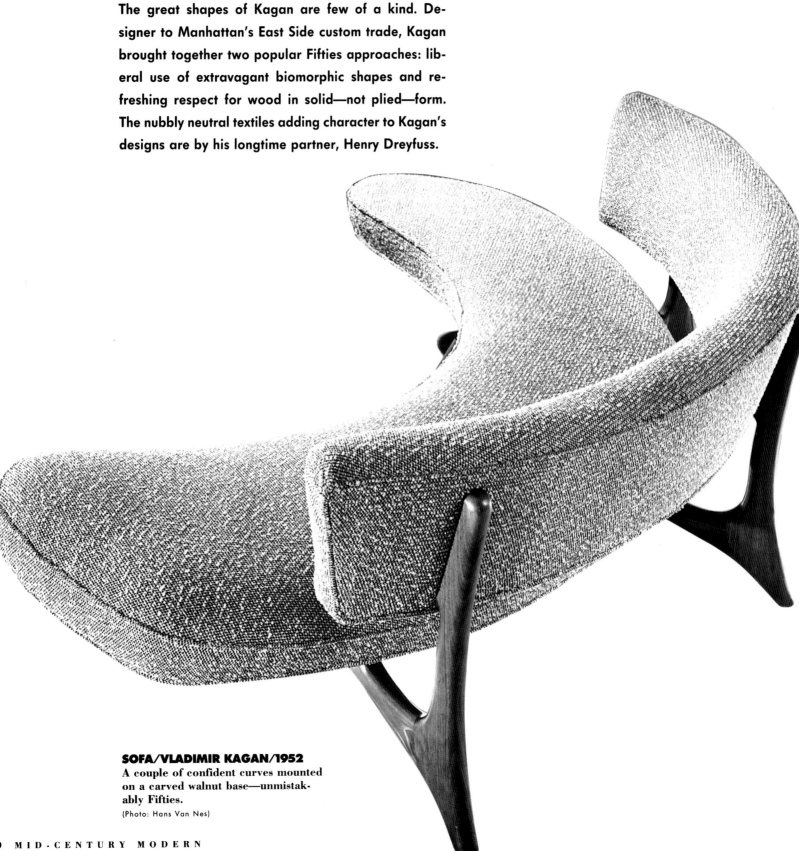

SOFA/VLADIMIR KAGAN/1952
A couple of confident curves mounted on a carved walnut base—unmistakably Fifties.

(Photo: Hans Van Nes)

(Photo: Hans Van Nes)

CHAIR/VLADIMIR KAGAN/1953
Shades of Art Nouveau, primarily handmade and fully hand-finished. Rich walnut legs, luxurious leather upholstery.

(Photo: Hans Van Nes)

TWO-SEATER/VLADIMIR KAGAN/1950s
Oddly animated for waiting-room furniture, the curvy leather cushions are separated by a discreet tabletop.

(Photo: Hans Van Nes)

CONTOUR LOUNGE CHAIR/VLADIMIR KAGAN/1955
A pleasing little chair with unassuming proportions, black-and-white chenille fabric over foam rubber upholstery.

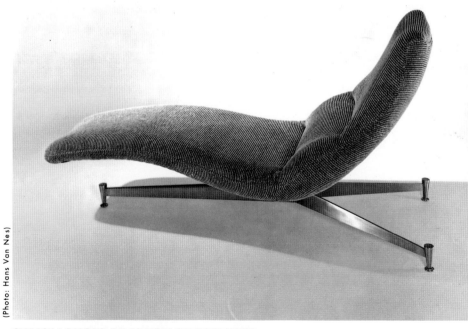

(Photo: Hans Van Nes)

CHAISE LONGUE/VLADIMIR KAGAN/1958
The contoured chaise, mounted on a stainless-steel tripod base, resembles later Italian offerings—ultrachic and a bit bizarre.

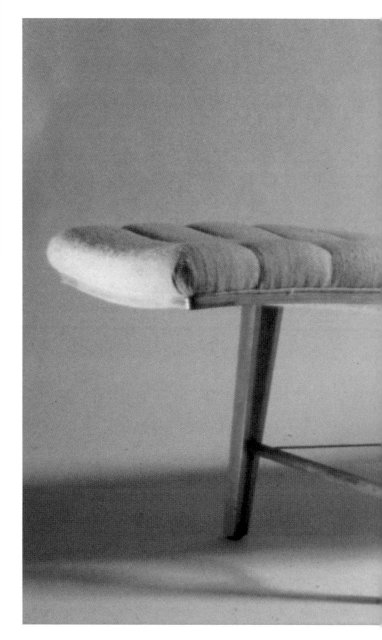

EDWARD WORMLEY

A welcome bastion of good design in the mass-market community, Ed Wormley turned out thousands of chairs, tables, wardrobes, and sofas for Dunbar of Indiana from the 1930s through the '50s, some in traditional styles, some modern. His best efforts look effortless in a well-crafted, almost Scandinavian way.

SEATING UNIT/VLADIMIR KAGAN/ 1950s

CHAISE/EDWARD WORMLEY/1947
Dubbed by Dunbar the Listen-to-Me couch, this chaise is made of unusually luxurious materials—white maple with American cherry legs, woolen upholstery, brass and copper wires crisscrossed for stability below.

CHAIR/EDWARD WORMLEY/1947
This graceful mahogany chair for Dunbar was suggested by a similar one designed in Dresden in the 1890s.

(Photos: Mark Meachem, The Liliane Stewart Collection, Le Château Dufresne, Musée des Arts Décoratifs de Montréal)

ISAMU NOGUCHI

A sculptor is a sculptor, even when working in the furniture medium. Isamu Noguchi's wide-ranging work on architectural panels, monumental outdoor projects, lighting, playground equipment, and toys freed him from preconceptions of what furniture ought to be.

LOW COFFEE TABLE/ISAMU NOGUCHI/1949

Only Noguchi could interpret table legs so freely. Four the same? How about three, a rudder-shaped one of plywood and two of aluminum outlining the same parabola. Lacquered and laminated in black, for Herman Miller.

TABLE/ISAMU NOGUCHI/c. 1954

A Japanese washbasin was the unlikely takeoff point for this unusual table for Knoll. A thoroughly modern compendium of materials: Formica, plywood, steel wire, Beaverboard, and cast iron all played roles.

JENS RISOM

For more than forty years a respected figure on the good design scene, Danish-born, New York-based Jens Risom designed furniture both for mass production and a custom trade.

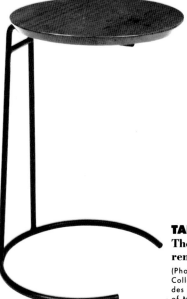

TABLE/JENS RISOM/c. 1951
The indispensable stacking side table, rendered in wrought iron and wood.

(Photo: Mark Meachem, The Liliane Stewart Collection, Le Château Dufresne, Musée des Arts Décoratifs de Montréal, gift of Mrs. Anne Hatfield Rothschild)

(Photo: Philadelphia Museum of Art: Purchased)

(Photo: The Brooklyn Museum)

LAMP/ISAMU NOGUCHI/c. 1945
For his sister, Noguchi created this symphony of simplicity—three wooden legs with a paper cylinder around them. Knoll produced it, but its lack of guile was its commercial downfall: unscrupulous entrepreneurs had a field day knocking it off.

ARMCHAIR/JENS RISOM/c. 1958
This low, slanted walnut-and-lacquer chair with its distorted-frequency muslin fabric was featured in 1958's Design for the Home show at The Brooklyn Museum.

WENDELL LOVETT

Seattle architect Wendell H. Lovett designed that which was needed to furnish his architectural commissions—mostly modern glass and stone houses on Puget Sound. All proclaimed an unabashed love of industrial fittings and machine-inspired forms.

(Photo: Wendell Lovett)

**SOFA WITH SPACE-FRAME BASE/
WENDELL LOVETT/1955**
Jet-age inspired, this sofa called
flashy attention to itself with untimid
angles and extreme triangular legs.

**TRANSPARENT ACRYLIC TABLE/
WENDELL LOVETT/1948**

➤ **FIREHOOD FIREPLACE/WENDELL
LOVETT/1953**

FLEXI-FIBRE CHAIR/WENDELL LOVETT/1952

Vulcanized plastic was steamed or dipped in hot water to make it stretch over the folding metal frame.

(Photo: Wendell Lovett)

FRAME OF DRAWERS/WENDELL LOVETT/1954

(Photo: Wendell Lovett)

(Photo: Wendell Lovett)

■A low-budget vacation house was fitted out with Lovett's advanced furniture designs—a 1956 sofa with wing back and space frame supports and 1952 flexi-fiber chairs.

(Photo: Wendell Lovett)

EERO SAARINEN

Of the mid-century furniture designers who were also architects, Eero Saarinen, Finnish-born son of architect Eliel Saarinen, made the biggest impression on the American landscape. Though he saw his courageous design statements rendered in concrete and steel—the great sweeping arch of the Yale University hockey rink "like an inverted Viking ship," the horizontal headquarters of the John Deere Company in Illinois "like a Japanese teahouse in raw steel"—he never lost interest in pursuing the essence of good, unified design in something as humble as a chair.

AMERICAN ORIGINALS

LAMP/A.W. & MARION GELLER/ c. 1950
Flying-saucer Fifties: this lamp used the reflector principle, very much in vogue, and a ball-tipped tripod base.

GRASSHOPPER CHAIR/EERO SAARINEN/1948
Saarinen's first chair for Knoll, of which Florence Knoll said, "It's a perfectly nice chair, but not one of the great successes." But hasn't it held up? The laminated bent plywood arm/ legs are a brilliant economy, still to be admired.

"ANYWHERE" LAMP/GRETA VON NESSEN/1952

Of enameled aluminum, this light-weight lamp was designed for maximum portability.

(Photo: Philadelphia Museum of Art)

FLOOR LAMP/GILBERT A. WATROUS/c. 1950

A top winner in The Museum of Modern Art's 1950 Lamp Design competition and the only one to remain in its permanent collection. Adjustable to virtually any position via a metal ball held in its socket by magnetism, through which passes the main stem. The conical shade is made of fiberglass.

(Photo: The Museum of Modern Art)

(Photo: The Museum of Modern Art)

LAMP/PHILIP JOHNSON & RICHARD KELLY/1950

A typically inventive design from the well-known architect. The light bulb is forsaken in favor of a dimmer unit that regulates the intensity of light coils inside the chrome cylinder. The peaked reflector catches the upward illumination and directs it out and down.

ALUMINUM CHAIRS/PAUL MCCOBB/ 1958
Why not aluminum? To draw attention to its potential, McCobb designed these humorously shaped chairs for the ALCOA Corporation's Forecast program in 1958. They were exhibited but never produced.

DESK/ANONYMOUS/1950s

The solid oak desk, made in America, takes a refreshing approach to the relationship between solid form and space.

(Photo: Tim Street-Porter/Fifty/50, New York)

(Photo: Tim Street-Porter/Fifty/50, New York)

COFFEE TABLE/ANONYMOUS/1950s

The guitar image is an apt one for the Fifties. This black lacquered coffee table with its string decoration and singular shape needs no designer's name to make it stand out as special. The geometric rug is from France, source of many great Fifties carpets.

(Photo: Mark Meachem, The Liliane Stewart Collection, Le Château Dufresne, Musée des Arts Décoratifs de Montréal, gift of Edgar Bartolucci)

BARWA CHAIR/EDGAR BARTOLUCCI & JACK WALDHEIM/1947

This is not a rocker. Its two positions—sitting and reclining—are achieved simply by shifting one's weight. Of lightweight tubular aluminum, slipcovered in canvas.

CLOCK ANONYMOUS/ 1950s

No other era dared to make clocks in such strange and wonderful shapes. The public lost no time in making weird wall clocks a Fifties fashion. This one, by the Howard Miller Clock Company of Michigan, is an outstanding example of the genre.

(Photo: Herman Miller)

SCOOP CHAIR AND TABLE/SOL BLOOM/1950

A display artist and tool maker, Sol Bloom, is behind this chair and table of woven steel mesh, marketed in the early '50s by a young New York group called Designed for Moderns.

CATCH-ALL/SOL BLOOM/1950

ROCKING CHAIR/RUSSELL WOODARD/c. 1958

A curvaceous rocker in wire mesh, designed for outdoor use, was the product of a small New York City manufacturer. It retailed for $36.

(Photo: The Brooklyn Museum)

(Photo: Maurice Martiné)

CHAIR/MAURICE MARTINÉ/1947

Another California entry with an appropriately nautical aspect: a steel-and-wood chair with yacht-cord seat and back.

(Photo: Julius Shulman)

LOUNGE CHAIRS AND TABLE/ HENRIK VAN KEPPEL & TAYLOR GREEN/1947

The Southern California team of Van Keppel and Green made outdoors as smart as indoors with a line of metal-framed seating pieces and tables strung with yacht cord and topped with opaque glass. For this and furniture made of redwood and rattan, they drew kudos from the international arbiters of good design.

THE DESIGNERS: THE EUROPEANS

fter several hundred years of quiescence in the furniture arts, Italy's emergence after World War II as a leader in the field came as a great surprise. From Milan, Italy's design nucleus, came furnishings with an overriding concern for style, expressed in the sculpted, curvilinear terms that had besotted the entire international design community.

But fortuitous couplings between designers and manufacturers gave Italy a creative edge. The relationships of manufacturer Cesare Cassina with Giò Ponti, Carlo de Carli, Ico Parisi, and Gianfranco Frattini exemplified the way in which Italian manufacturers were willing to risk investment in unusual designs and were able to do so because of small-scale production. Oswaldo Borsani and Tecno, Marco Zanuso and Arflex, Franco Albini and Poggi, were other fruitful alliances that resulted in the unerring execution of forward-looking designs.

France's strength in the 1950s was in the decoration of complete interiors. French designers such as Jacques Dumond, Ramos, and Gautier gained fame pulling together modern rooms with colorful aplomb, often using imported pieces from the more avant-garde designers of the United States.

Native furniture in France tended to rely heavily on novelties, and there were sweeping vogues for saddle-stitched animal hide, basketwork, and black wrought iron. Individual pieces of lasting import were rare, and no distinct, unified "look" developed in France in the 1950s. At the end of the decade, French furniture design picked up steam and went on to field the playful, innovative 1960s with greater success.

DESK/ITALIAN/c. 1955
CHAIR/ITALIAN/c. 1955
LAMP/FRENCH/1950s
VASES/ITALIAN/1950s
Black-painted tubular steel and bright baked-enamel colors link the straightforward desk, made by the firm of Arteluce, and the chair with its trajectory curves. The lamp—three different shades on wall-mounted rods—disregards convention in a spirited European way. The heavy-walled vases are typical of the Italian Fifties look in hand-blown glass.

(Photo: Tim Street-Porter)

LADY CHAIR/MARCO ZANUSO/ 1951

After World War II, the Pirelli Company presented architect Marco Zanuso with samples of a new material —foam rubber—and asked him to investigate possible applications. The result was the Lady armchair, with its broad seat, free-form armrests and informal upholstery pattern.

(Photo: Arflex)

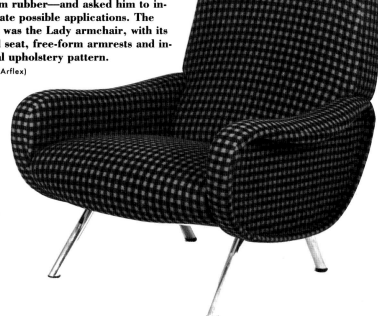

ARMCHAIR/GIANFRANCO FRATTINI/ 1955

The urbane Italian armchair was a specialty of the Milanese firm of Cassina, here shown in a conservative but still stylish guise.

(Photo: Cassina)

FIORENZA CHAIR/FRANCO ALBINI/ 1953

A wing chair for the airline age. Padded foam-rubber seat, back, and arms are mounted on a supporting X-frame of gracefully articulated wood.

(Photo: Arflex)

ELETTRA CHAIR/B.B.P.R./1954

This elegant middleweight side chair resulted from the spare conjunction of bent metal rods and padded planks of wood.

(Photo: Arflex)

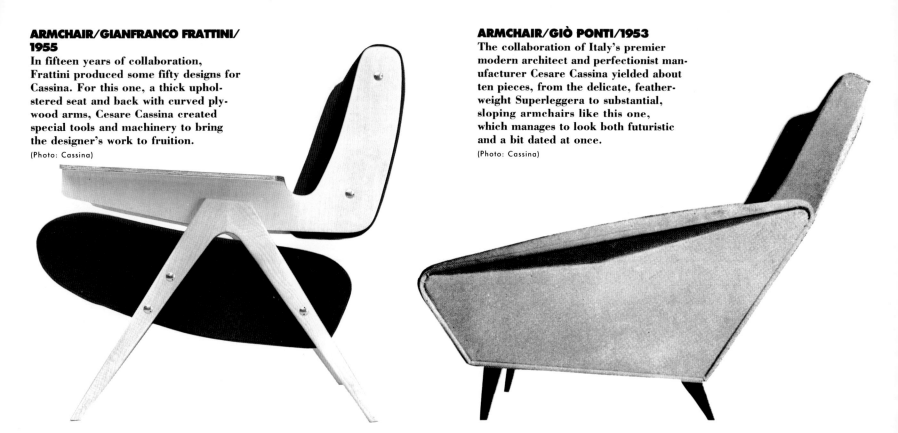

ARMCHAIR/GIANFRANCO FRATTINI/ 1955

In fifteen years of collaboration, Frattini produced some fifty designs for Cassina. For this one, a thick upholstered seat and back with curved plywood arms, Cesare Cassina created special tools and machinery to bring the designer's work to fruition.

(Photo: Cassina)

ARMCHAIR/GIÒ PONTI/1953

The collaboration of Italy's premier modern architect and perfectionist manufacturer Cesare Cassina yielded about ten pieces, from the delicate, featherweight Superleggera to substantial, sloping armchairs like this one, which manages to look both futuristic and a bit dated at once.

(Photo: Cassina)

(Photo: Cassina)

COUCH AND ARMCHAIRS/ICO PARISI/1954

In the search for new forms, Parisi came up with these clean-curved shapes, round and ovoid upholstered forms sliced on the diagonal and raised off the floor on short, tapered legs.

(Photo: Tim Street-Porter/Downtown, New York)

TABLE/ITALIAN/1950s

A great pair of rosewood legs, splayed for stability and also for style. This type of inverted V table leg was a particularly Italian reflection of worldwide interest in sculptural form.

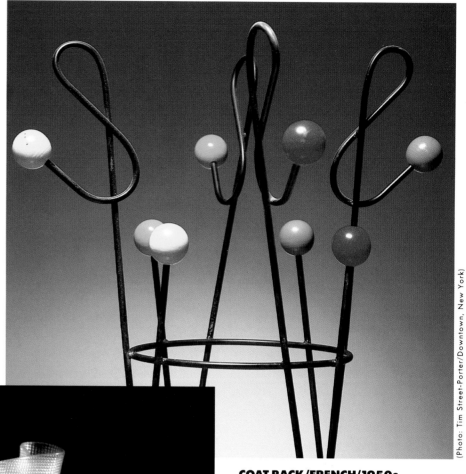

(Photo: Tim Street-Porter/Downtown, New York)

COAT RACK/FRENCH/1950s

Another Fifties science project. Hall stands and coat racks of black wrought iron, twisted to look like G clefs with wooden nuclei, were ubiquitous in postwar France.

(Photo: The Brooklyn Museum)

VASE/FLUVIO BIANCONI/c. 1950

The essence of mid-century free-form frozen in glass. The handkerchief-type vase was a popular form indigenous to Italy. Hand blown, no two were ever exactly alike, in shape or in decoration.

LIVING ROOM/ L. MIRABAUD/ c. 1958

Elements bridging the Fifties and Sixties come together in this crisp, urbane environment. The deep half-circle chair and the colorful squares of felt-covered foam on the floor pave the way to Pop. The Noguchi table, rattan chaise, and cantilevered standing lamp were French Fifties favorites.

CARLO MOLLINO ROOM/1950

Which is more outrageous, the sculpted forms of the wooden chairs and daybed, with their frankly exposed rivets, the painted rushing-river mural, or Mollino's luxuriously striated, mirrored interpretation of a functional storage wall? An installation at The Brooklyn Museum's Italy at Work show of 1950–51.

DESK/JEAN PROUVÉ/1952
CHAIR/RAMOS/1950s
LAMP/SERGE MOUILLE/1950s

Metal legs like the points of a draftsman's compass and a sleekly curved top in two parallel curves characterize the desk, which is simple but refined in contrast to the hearty geometrics of the chair.

CHAIR/PIERRE PAULIN/1954

Continuous steel rod legs and a square leather basket of a seat. An early entry from a designer who was to become one of the Pop furniture sculptors of the Sixties.

▶ SUPERLEGGERA CHAIR/GIÒ PONTI/ 1957

The Superleggera is a timeless classic evoking another timeless classic, the American Shaker chair. Cassina, the manufacturer calibrated and modified the prototype until it was virtually perfect—a wonder of lightness and strength.

**CHAISE LONGUE/FRENCH/1950s
COFFEE TABLE/T.H. ROBSJOHN-
GIBBINGS/EARLY 1940s
FLOOR LAMP/LIGHTOLIER/1950s
CARPET/FRENCH/1950s**

The sensuous lounge wittily pairs
solidly turned peg legs with the infor-
mality of canvas lashed to tubular
steel—a revelation of French chic,
underscored by a geometric wool car-
pet of uncertain heritage. The pro-
nouncedly free-form glass-topped
table was made by American manufacturer Widdicomb; the three-part standing lamp, madly successful and much
imitated, by Lightolier of New Jersey.

(Photo: Tim Street-Porter/Alan Moss Gallery, New York)

CHAIR/ITALIAN/1950s
LAMPS/ISABELLE GIANPIETRO/1956
Airplane-seating angles and vertically striped fabric are recurring themes
in Italian upholstered furniture of the 1950s. Their shapes are somewhat dis-
tant from today's taste, yet not enough to look quaint. The all-glass lamps
light a prescient path toward Sixties neomodernism.

STUDY/A. GUENOT/c. 1958

The light, airy atmosphere of this urbane study is enhanced by polished ash built-ins, cane chairs, and cork-lined walls.

FLOOR LAMP/FRENCH/1950s

A lighting fixture unlike any other, it resembles a praying mantis in perpetually tense balance between the thick and thin parts of the modeled wood and the volume of the suspended globe.

(Photo: Tim Street-Porter/Downtown, New York)

BAR/ITALIAN/1950s

Happy hour on the Via Veneto. Spiky wrought-iron legs reappear above a three-part plywood cabinet and end in a curved marble counter. Stylized painted decoration resembles American Fifties cocktail-lounge graphics.

(Photo: Tim Street-Porter/Downtown, New York)

THE DESIGNERS: THE SCANDINAVIANS

A study in form: two radically different designs from the imagination of the same designer. With cotton string work on a minimal frame of metal, the lounge on the left is a playful splay of angles. Rarer is the three-legged chair in beech veneer, painted black. It's only two pieces of form-pressed wood: the back and front leg are one, the seat and rear legs the other.

For the Scandinavian furniture designers, the 1950s were years of international triumph. Their output, which took the best of handcrafted and machine approaches and blended them seamlessly, became synonymous with good taste and high quality. It ranged in demeanor from serious—such as Hans Wegner's sturdy, elemental chairs—to lighthearted, even frivolous, like the heart- and cone-shaped chairs of Verner Panton and the swollen egg shapes of Arne Jacobsen.

In the late 1940s, the Scandinavians leaned heavily on wood—Aalto on birch ply, Wegner and Finn Juhl on walnut—but it was teak, imported, ironically, from the Philippines, that became most closely identified with the Scandinavian countries. Jacobsen, Panton, and Poul Kjaerholm also spoke the international language of metal and plastics, thus departing from Danish craft traditions but never losing sight of pared-down functionalism and unpretentious good looks.

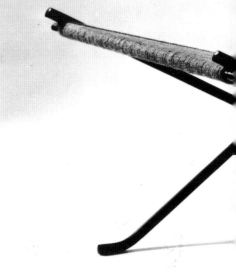

TABLE/FINN JUHL/1950
A serviceable surface rendered in subtle sculptural detail.
(Photo: Philadelphia College of Art Collection)

(Photo: Louis Poulsen)

"Dear craftsmen friends! Throw away your artists' berets and bow ties and get into overalls. Down with artistic pretentiousness! Simply make things that are fit for use: That is enough to keep you busy, and you will sell vast quantities and make lots of money."

POUL HENNINGSEN

► LOUNGE CHAIR/BRUNO MATHSSON/1934

A classic doesn't jar you into submission, it seduces you with style. Mathsson's sensuous lounge chair actually dates from '34, but its ergonomic form, beech laminations, and webbed upholstery became touchstones of Fifties design. A Swedish classic, still in production in numerous variations.

(Photo: Mathsson International)

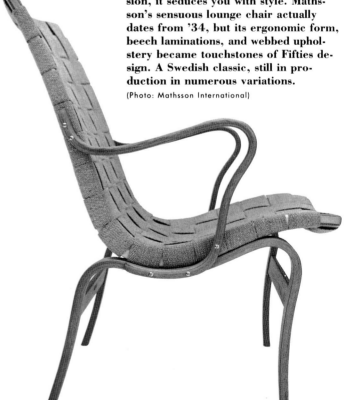

► PH-5 LAMP/POUL HENNINGSEN/1957

Danish lighting-design genius Henningsen concerned himself with the relationship between people's true needs and the honest functioning of their everyday equipment. The PH-5 was the culmination of a thirty-year search for an efficient, no-glare fixture. The by-product was classic style in a future tense. It will be at least a hundred years before the PH-5 looks antique. Made by Louis Poulsen, Copenhagen, in four colors: red, blue, white, and lavender.

CHAIRS AND TABLE/PETER HVIDT & ORLA MØLGAARD-NIELSEN/ c. 1958

Fruitful joint efforts of these architect/cabinetmakers did much to popularize Danish mass-produced furniture. The laminate gluing process was borrowed from tennis racquets, the X legs from Miës's Barcelona chair.

(Photo: Fritz Hansen)

CREDENZA/ARNE VODDER/1950s

A case for the goods—long, low, and lively. Sliding doors, drawers, and drop-down panel conceal a multitude of clutter within a sleek exterior.

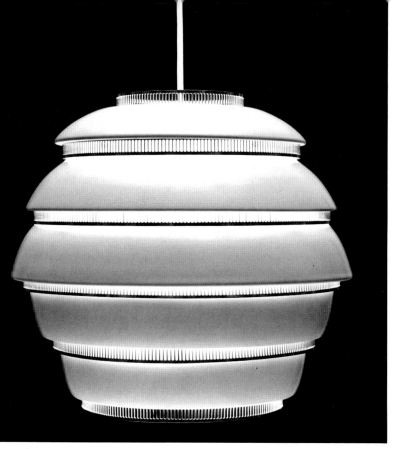

DINING TABLE AND CHAIRS/ARNE JACOBSEN/1957

All-wood legs increased the formality of the broad-shouldered stacking chair over metal-legged variations. The table is a model of simplicity, stability, and good taste.

(Photo: Fritz Hansen)

➤ **HANGING LAMP/ALVAR AALTO/ 1951**

Aalto's contributions in Finland ranged from city planning and the design of factories, homes, and exhibition pavillions to furniture, textiles, glass, and lighting. This stepped globular fixture of brass and white-painted aluminum has been in continuous production for more than thirty years.

(Photo: Philadelphia Museum of Art)

LOUNGE CHAIRS/ALF SVENSSON/ c. 1955

Jet-line design, remarkably like the seating in a 747, yet quite radical for its time.

(Photo: Fritz Hansen)

LOUNGE CHAIR/POUL KJAERHOLM/ 1951

The well-tempered chair: an early Kjaerholm experiment in tempered steel. Legs, side pieces, and uprights are all cut from a single piece of metal.

(Photo: Fritz Hansen)

ARMCHAIR/FINN JUHL/1951

The most sculptural of the Danes, Juhl's chair is a play of right-angled cross members and floating free-forms. For Baker, a Grand Rapids, Michigan, manufacturer.

(Photo: Philadelphia Museum of Art: Gift of Mr. and Mrs. N. Richard Miller)

STACKING CHAIRS/HANS WEGNER/ c. 1949

Wegner is the foremost figure in the postwar revival of Danish cabinetry. His consummate craft is proof of his belief that furniture should not be designed, but made. A stacking version of one of his meticulous chairs for Fritz Hansen.

(Photo: Fritz Hansen)

SWAN CHAIR/ARNE JACOBSEN/ 1957

The showy Swan in an uncommon incarnation: bent plywood legs replacing the usual metal base.

(Photo: Fritz Hansen)

(Photo: Fritz Hansen)

SIDE CHAIR/ARNE JACOBSEN/1958

From the man who gave us the Egg chair came this scooped-out yolk of a seat. There is a kind of whiz-bang humor to Jacobsen's designs that is sheer delight.

CONE CHAIR/VERNER PANTON/1959

Another northern light, Verner Panton was obsessed with the single-form chair throughout his career. His revolving cone was the perfect exclamation point to a space-age interior.

(Photo: Louis Schnakenburg)

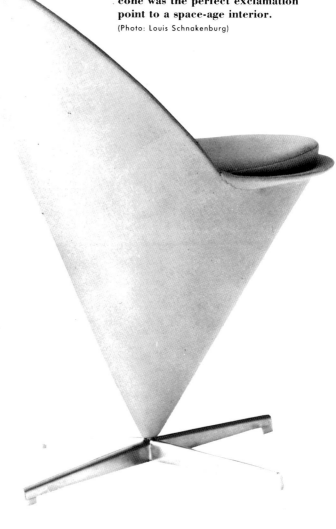

WIRE CONE CHAIR/VERNER PANTON/1959

Panton admits his chairs rarely have four legs "because the processing of new materials . . . calls for new shapes." But the wire frame of this chair recalls nothing more esoteric than a hoopskirt.

(Photo: Louis Schnakenburg)

➤ STACKING CHAIRS/ARNE JACOBSEN/1955
Never out of production since their debut, Jacobsen's all-purpose, free-form stacking chairs are available in a rainbow of intense colors.

LIVING A FIFTIES FANTASY

ne could hardly mistake the homes on the following pages for period interiors. Though the furnishings date from the Fifties, their colorful juxtaposition, managed with the hindsight of three decades, is an audacious, loving send-up of that era. These contemporary revisions of the look of the mid-century say as much about the style and sentimentality of the current age as they do about the time that inspired them.

SUBURBAN URBAN

"Bringing the outdoors in" was a popular architectural strategem in the Fifties, an impulse that made good sense when the surroundings were bucolic or, at least, suburban woodsy. Live trees growing up through the floor of a house and out the roof were not unknown. Walls of glass blurred the distinction between inside and out, with foliage becoming the backdrop for the furnishings. Flagstone and brick were brought indoors for the warmth and textural interest they could provide.

In this New York City loft, located on a block heavily trafficked by trucks, the same materials used in the 1950s to bring the outdoors in were called upon to perform exactly the opposite function: to keep it out. The ploy is surprisingly effective.

The raw material was a typical, unextraordinary loft space—long and narrow, with windows at each end, a dark central core, and a string of Corinthian columns harking back to the building's nineteenth century construction. The loft's owner is a well-known painter with a predilection for the furniture of the decade in which he was born. His collection, including pieces by Marco Zanuso, Carlo Mollino, Charles Eames, and George Nelson, sat in storage, awaiting a conducive setting.

Architect Christian Hubert created virtually a new house within the raw loft space, using an unexpected combination of materials reminiscent of a 1950s suburban home. Sliding glass doors lead to a bedroom instead of a patio, still creating the suggestion of outdoor space and admitting light into the dark interior. Slabs of flagstone imbedded in cement are a wonderfully craggy contrast with the smoothness of new Sheetrock walls. The Victorian columns, structural necessities running the entire length of the space, were sheathed in flaring cylinders of concrete and given a twentieth-century expression.

The result is not a narrow "period" re-creation, but an insulated environment, acoustically and psychologically removed from the gritty urbanity of the outside world.

■The design for living in the loft's main space incorporates Wendell Lovett's Firehood fireplace on a specially constructed concrete platform, Zanuso chairs, and anonymous tables, rug, and cabinet.

(Photo: Tim Street-Porter)

(Photo: Tim Street-Porter)

■Carlo Mollino's cloven-hoof
chair in metal-studded white vinyl, the
1952 "Anywhere" lamp of Greta von
Nessen, and an Eames-style plywood
cabinet occupy a corner of the bedroom.

■ Central to the loft's main living
area are the unfamiliar shapes of Marco
Zanuso's 1951 molded foam rubber
"Lady" chairs, a rare sight in the States.

■Dining is done in what seems a space-
age café: Knoll's popsicle table,
Eames wire chairs, and a starburst chandelier stand out against a backdrop of
corrugated, perforated metal walls.

(Photo: Tim Street-Porter)

(Photo: Tim Street-Porter)

■Arne Jacobsen's swan in its large sofa form is bathed in mauve light from an overhead fixture.

STANDING LAMP/1950s
Maximum adjustability was a hallmark of Fifties lighting. This one with its unmatched metal shades is typically free-swinging.

■Dwarfed by a forest of columns are the graceful Antelope chairs of Ernest Race, surviving reminders of the 1951 Festival of Britain.

GOOD DESIGN IN KITSCH

Los Angeles is a Fifties' city if ever there was one. A typical Angeleno of the 1950s, according to lore, hopped into a two-tone Chevy with rocket fins and cruised past drive-in coffee shops with futuristic jutting roofs and flickering neon signs until it was time to take a dip in a kidney-shaped swimming pool.

Los Angeles has its landmarks of serious modern architecture, but it is also endowed with homes that represent the popular culture of the period. Allee Willis, a songwriter, has one. It actually dates from 1937, when it was built by M-G-M as a "party house." A stucco classic of streamlined modern architecture, it features a see-through view, turrets along the roofline, and round, hexagonal, and octagonal rooms. In this fantasy of Hollywood's heyday, Ms. Willis has created her own fantasy, which can best be described as top-quality kitsch.

Outside, the fantasy is ongoing, with lush landscaping, a swimming pool, and a collection of marbleized bowling balls sunk in sand to create a "moon walk."

(Photos: Tim Street-Porter)

(Photo: Tim Street-Porter)

■The living room couches, reclaimed after years in an out-of-business uphol-stery shop, were recovered in nubbly pink fabric with black and gold threads. The two-piece sectional has an elasticized pocket at the back for magazines. The coffee table is an American boomerang, unsigned; the blond hi-fi console a Grundig; and the TV a Sylvania Halovision from 1951, so called because the white frame around the screen lights up.

■Overlooking the pool is a wrought-iron bar with a boomerang-shaped top of turquoise, gold, black, and coral mosaic tile, and African figu-rines mounted on the front.

(Photos: Tim Street-Porter)

■The flotsam and jetsam of Fifties popular culture have a room of their own, anchored by an unusual interstate rug.

■Fifties furnishings segue into new-music technology: an Eames shell at the organ, a flying-saucer standing lamp, and a diagonal blond desk of obscure origins.

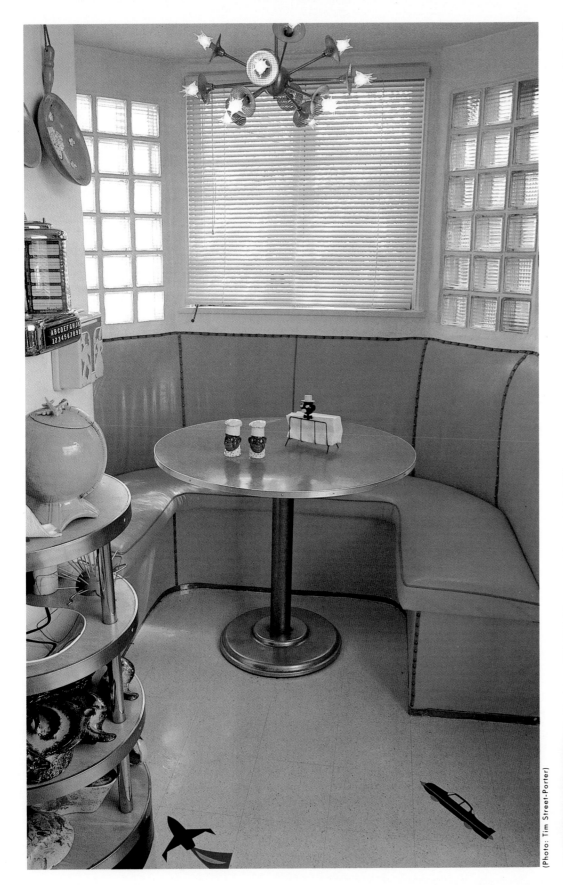

■The glass block windowed niche, the pink vinyl banquette, and the half-round Formica counter date back to the time of the house's construction in the late 1930s.

■Colorful anodized aluminum tumblers are to collectors of Fifties kitchenware what Depression glass is to collectors of Thirties tableware.

(Photo: Tim Street-Porter)

(Photo: Tim Street-Porter)

LIVING A FIFTIES FANTASY **149**

PORT OF PINK

The exterior arrests you with its persuasive pink brick and jutting angles, and the interior follows through on its promise. Photographer Graham Henman's Los Angeles house makes full, florid use of all the Fifties trademarks: interior stone walls, mosaic tiles, terrazzo floors, recessed lighting or three-in-a-row hanging lamps, furniture with spindly wrought iron legs.

(Photos: Tim Street-Porter)

(Photos: Tim Street-Porter)

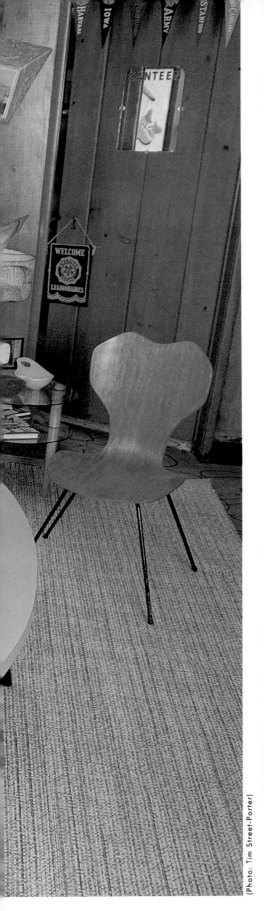

■Only the pine-paneled "rec" room, with its ersatz leopard-skin upholstered rattan couch and Formica free-form coffee table, crosses the border into kitsch. The pink-and-black kitchen and bathroom are period classics.

EL RANCHO DELUXE

This Los Angeles vision-in-turquoise was a good shot at the American dream when it was owner-built in 1947. Its recent occupants, Alan and Lori Erenberg, found its suburban spaces the perfect showcase for their collection of flamboyant Fifties furnishings.

■Even the car parked outside, a rare 1957 Dual Ghia by Chrysler, is a clue to the comprehensive collecting compulsions of the people who live inside.

(Photo: Tim Street-Porter)

(Photo: Tim Street-Porter)

■Ample evidence abounds of a fondness for fiberglass-shaded lamps in odd shapes, and for the colors of the Fifties fashion palette—salmon pink, forest green, and, of course, turquoise.

■The living room couch, in curvaceous Hollywood boudoir style, is covered in magenta chintz with a pattern of tiny *vermicelli* squiggles.

(Photo: Tim Street-Porter)

(Photo: Tim Street-Porter)

(Photo: Tim Street-Porter)

(Photo: Tim Street-Porter)

■In the kitchen, nostalgia by no other name: speckled linoleum on the floor, a starburst chandelier, an upholstered vinyl banquette, a Formica and chrome dinette, even a period gas range.

■The dining table is definitely Noguchi-influenced. The chairs, of chartreuse vinyl, are by American maker Thonet. The copper ceiling fixture was a do-it-yourself project from a 1952 decorating book.

■Unsigned, but never mind: The extravagantly angled armchair and blondwood cabinet are still great finds. The light source in the standing lamp is in the base; the tilting full moon of fiberglass serves only as a reflector.

BROADWAY VIDEO

High above Times Square in New York, the owners of Broadway Video, a videotape editing facility whose electronic heart comprises the very latest equipment, have chosen to furnish its common spaces with mid-century classics. The feeling, obviously, is that they have made the translation into the high-technology '80s with no loss of design credibility.

The lounge features, besides a pool table, Harry Bertoia's diamond chairs and the inexpensive, readily available and forever chic chairs known variously as Hardoy, butterfly, or sling. The glass-topped coffee table with wrought iron legs and the geometric wool rug are newly made. They were designed by Nord Haggerty, a New York designer.

The projection TV in the conference room is viewed from the enduring comfort of Arne Jacobsen stacking chairs in white, a 1955 design that has been in uninterrupted production. Coffee is served from a big-wheeled Alvar Aalto cart, another still-in-production piece that made its debut at the 1939 New York World's Fair.

(Photo: Tim Street-Porter)

(Photo: Tim Street-Porter)

THE ECLECTIC EYE

The inhabitant of this high-ceilinged space, newly hatched out of one of New York's former factories, is the owner of a Greenwich Village store through which pass some of the most exemplary furniture, fittings and fixtures of the Fifties. Suzanne Lipschutz's pioneering sensibilities pervade her private space as well. She shies away from the obvious, seeks out the unexpected, takes chances with the dubiously tasteful, and pulls it all together with panache.

(Photo: Tim Street-Porter)

■The Italian parchment table with its curling edges by Aldo Tura of Milan is undeniably unique. The one-of-a-kind rug it sits on is a take-off on the lines and forms of Miró.

(Photo: Tim Street-Porter)

■Verner Panton's cone chair in brilliant orange sits atop a European op art rug.

(Photo: Tim Street-Porter)

■Emblematic Fifties: a wrought iron and plaster composite wall sconce, with a ballerina theme, made by Frederick Weinberg.

■The tall back chairs and glass-topped, lacquered base coffee table are typical of the tastes of designer James Mont's clientele. The wooden room divider is a department store display piece, the trompe l'oeil marble wallpaper vintage Fifties

(Photo: Tim Street-Porter/Fifty/50, New York)

BACK TO BLACK

In this living room setting, an oriental serenity is accomplished with classics of the period, George Nelson's slat benches and cabinet, late '40s for Herman Miller; wrought-iron bar stools; and an anonymous couch, typically long, low, and flat.

(Photos: Bruce Osborne)

TOKYO STORY

A Japanese rock band lives here: who else? This is no longer Mid-Century Modern. It is a New Wave refraction of what the American Fifties looked like, seen from the opposite side of the world thirty years hence. None of the furniture is documented, and only some of it is period, but nevertheless, the vision is powerful.

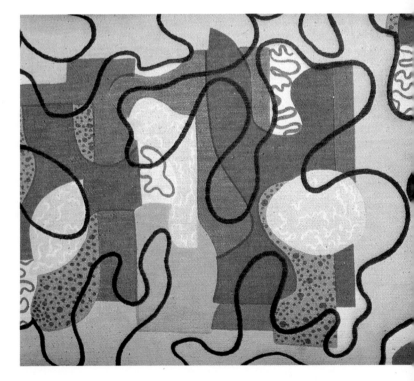

(Photos: Bruce Osborne)

■Outrageous optical effects pop out and take over center stage. The op effects are Sixties in inspiration, but the lines of the furniture are Fifties all the way.

SOURCE GUIDE

Retail Stores

ARIZONA

Do Wah Diddy
3642 E. Thomas Road
Phoenix, AZ 85018
(602) 957-3874

Shabooms
5533 W. Glendale
Glendale, AZ 85301
(602) 842-8687

CALIFORNIA

AD/50
601 Laguna Street
San Francisco, CA 94102
(415) 626-4575

Another Time
1586 Market Street
San Francisco, CA 94102
(415) 553-8900

Boomerang for Modern
3795 Park Blvd.
San Diego, CA 92103
(619) 295-1953

Cadillac Jack
2820 Gilroy Street
Los Angeles, CA 90039
(800) 775-5078

Centrium Furnishings
2166 Market Street
San Francisco, CA 94114
(415) 863-4195

Deco to 50s
149 Gough
San Francisco, CA 94102
(415) 553-4500

Fat Chance
162 North LaBrea Avenue
Los Angeles, CA 90036
(213) 930-1960

Futurama
7956 Beverly Blvd.
Los Angeles, CA 90048
(213) 651-5767

Jet Age
250 Oak Street
San Francisco, CA 94102
(415) 864-1950

Kuhlhaus
5259 Melrose Avenue
Los Angeles, CA 90038
(213) 962-6210

Modern Era Decor
1797 Market Street
San Francisco, CA 94103
(415) 431-8599

Modern Times
338 North LaBrea Avenue
Los Angeles, CA 90036
(213) 930-1150

Modernica
7366 Beverly Blvd.
Los Angeles, CA 90036
(213) 933-0383

Skank World
7205 Beverly Blvd.
Los Angeles, CA 90036
(213) 939-7858

20th Century Furnishings
1612 Market Street
San Francisco, CA 94102
(415) 626-0542

Vintage Modern
182 Gough Street
San Francisco, CA 94102
(415) 861-8162

X-21
2409 21st Street
Sacramento, CA 95818
(916) 731-5505

COLORADO

Atomic Antiques
56 S. Broadway
Denver, CO 80209
(303) 722-0530

FLORIDA

Art Moderne
1702 East 7th Avenue
Tampa, FL 33605
(813) 247-4450

Decades a Go Go
1514 East 7th Avenue
Tampa, FL 33605
(813) 248-2849

Modernism Gallery
1622 Ponce De Leon Blvd.
Coral Gables, FL 33134
(305) 442-8743

Senzatempo
815 Washington Avenue
Miami Beach, FL 33139
1-800-408-8419

Well Designed
6554 SW 40th Street
Miami, FL 33155
(305) 661-1386

ILLINOIS

**Richard Wright at
John Toomey Gallery**
818 North Blvd.
Oak Park, IL 60301
(707) 383-5234

Mid Century
642-1/2 West Addison
Chicago, IL 60613
(312) 549-5405

Modern Times
1508 N. Milwaukee
Chicago, IL 60622
(312) 772-8871

1945
225 West Huron
Chicago, IL 60610
(312) 573-1945

Urban Artifacts
2928 North Lincoln
Chicago, IL 60657
(312) 404-1008

Verve
3854 N. Lincoln
Chicago, IL 60613
(312) 348-7540

Zig Zag
3419 N. Lincoln Avenue
Chicago, IL 60657
(312) 525-1060

INDIANA

Rare Form
650 East Kessler
Indianapolis, IN 46220
(317) 357-6065

MARYLAND

Modern One
8 East Franklin St.
Baltimore, MD 21202
1-800-823-0090

MASSACHUSETTS

Ellipse
427 Main Street
Dennis, MA 02638
(508) 385-8626

Gumshoe
40 South Street
Boston, MA 02130
(617) 522-5066

Machine Age
354 Congress Street
Boston, MA 02210
(617) 482-0048

Pastiche
85 Harding Street
Worcester, MA 01604
(508) 756-1229

MICHIGAN

First 1/2
25 North Saginaw
Pontiac, MI
(313) 886-3443

Rage of the Age
220 S. Fourth Avenue
Ann Arbor, MI 48104
(313) 662-0777

Triola's
1494 Lake Lansing Road
Lansing, MI 48912
(517) 484-3480

NEW JERSEY

Of Rare Vintage
718 Cookman Avenue
Asbury Park, NJ 07712
(908) 988-9459

O'Vale
276 Norwood Avenue
Deal, NJ 07723
(908) 517-1573

NEW YORK

A+J 20th Century Designs
255 Lafayette Street
New York, NY 10012
(212) 226-6290

Amazon
240 Lafayette Street
New York, NY 10012
(212) 343-9415

Art & Industrial Design Shop
399 Lafayette Street
New York, NY 10012
(212) 477-0116

Atomic Passion
430 East 9th Street
New York, NY 10009
(212) 533-0718

Charles Brown
6 Lower Trinity Pass Road
Pound Ridge, NY 10576
(914) 764-8392

Citybarn Antiques
362 Atlantic Avenue
Brooklyn, NY 11217
(718) 855-8566

Donzella
90 East 10th Street
New York, NY 10003
(212) 598-9675

Full House
133 Wooster Street
New York, NY 10012
(212) 529-2298

Lin Weinberg
84 Wooster Street
New York, NY 10012
(212) 219-3022

1950
440 Lafayette Street
New York, NY 10012
(212) 995-1950

phoof
388 Bleecker Street
New York, NY 10014
(212) 807-1332

280 Modern
280 Lafayette Street
New York, NY 10012
(212) 941-5825

OHIO

Byrd/Braman
2882 Wasson Road
Cincinnati, OH 45209
(513) 631-8090

Go Modern
7426 Lorain Avenue
Cleveland, OH 44102
(216) 651-4590

Just 50s
3742 Kellogg Avenue
Cincinnati, OH 45206
(513) 221-1959

Studio Moderne
13006 Larchmere
Cleveland, OH 44120
(216) 721-2274

Suite Lorain
7105 Lorain Avenue
Cleveland, OH 44102
(216) 281-1959

OKLAHOMA

Elektra
4327 N. Western
Oklahoma City, OK 73118
(405) 524-4327

PENNSYLVANIA

Mode Moderne
159 N. 3rd Street
Philadelphia, PA 19106
(215) 627-0299

Streamlined Style
9 N. Madison Street
Allentown, PA 18102
(215) 433-4705

RHODE ISLAND

Off Broadway
432 Broadway
Providence, RI 02909
(401) 274-3150

TENNESSEE

Fever
113 Gay Street
Knoxville, TN 37902
(615) 525-4771

Flashback
2304 Central Avenue
Memphis, TN 38104
(901) 272-2304

TEXAS

Collage
3107 Routh Street
Dallas, TX 75201
(214) 880-0020

VIRGINIA

Daniel Donnelly Decorative Arts
107 N. Fayette
Alexandria, VA 22314
(703) 549-4672

WASHINGTON, DC

Eclectic
1918 18th Street N.W.
Washington, DC 20009
(202) 232-4207

Millennium
1528 U Street N.W.
Washington, DC 20009
(202) 483-1218

Manufacturers and Distributors

Design Selections International
PO Box 809
Croton-on-Hudson, NY 10520
(914) 271-3736
Fax: (914) 271-3793

Finn Juhl
Poul Kjaerholm
Hans Wegner

Herman Miller
PO Box 302
855 East Main Avenue
Zeeland, MI 49464
(800) 646-4400

Charles Eames
George Nelson
Isamu Noguchi

ICF
305 East 63rd Street
New York, NY 10021
(212) 750-0900
Fax: (212) 593-1152

Alvar Aalto
Poul Kjaerholm

Vladimir Kagan Design Group
1185 Park Avenue
New York, NY 10028
(212) 289-0031
Fax: (212) 360-7307

Vladimir Kagan

Knoll International
105 Wooster Street
New York, NY 10012
(212) 343-4000
Fax: (212) 343-4170

Harry Bertoia
Marcel Breuer
Eero Saarinen
Ludwig Miës van der Rohe

Scandinavian Design
127 East 59th Street
New York, NY 10022
(212) 755-6078
Fax: (212) 888-3928

Hans Wegner
Bruno Mathsson

Vitra
30-20 Thompson Avenue
Long Island City, NY 11101
(718) 472-1820
Fax: (718) 472-1825

Charles Eames

INDEX